101

SUPERSHOTS

······························

101 SUPERSHOTS

EVERY GOLFER'S GUIDE
TO LOWER SCORES

CHI CHI RODRIGUEZ WITH
JOHN ANDRISANI

ILLUSTRATED BY DOM LUPO

 Harper Perennial
A Division of HarperCollins*Publishers*

This book is dedicated to the Golf Writers of America. When my game deserted me, they didn't. For that, I will always be grateful.

A hardcover edition of this book was published in 1990 by Harper & Row, Publishers.

First HarperPerennial edition published 1991.

Designed by Helene Berinsky

The Library of Congress has catalogued the hardcover edition as follows:

Rodriguez, Chi Chi.
     101 supershots: every golfer's guide to lower scores/Chi Chi Rodriguez, with John Andrisani.—1st ed.
          p.   cm.
     ISBN 0-06-016264-3
     1. Golf.   I. Andrisani, John.   II. Title.   III. Title. One hundred one supershots.   IV. Title: One hundred and one supershots.
GV965.R567   1990
796.352'3—dc20   89-45709

ISBN 0-06-092070-X (pbk.)

91 92 93 94 95 DT/RRD 10 9 8 7 6 5 4 3 2 1

CONTENTS

3: OFF THE FAIRWAY   72

4: AROUND THE GREEN   108

5: ON THE GREEN   166

ACKNOWLEDGMENTS

The writing of this book, like a good marriage or a win on the Senior Tour, with my caddy at my side, was a team effort.

Special thanks go to John Andrisani, the senior instruction editor of *Golf* magazine, who so aptly presented my tips in an easy-to-follow technical language, so that every golfer would be able to learn them in practice quickly and apply them in play.

I'm also grateful to Dom Lupo, whose wonderfully lucid drawings make it possible for any golfer to see a particular shot come to life on the page and in his mind's eye.

Last, but by no means least, I'm honored that Jack Nicklaus, a good friend who just happens to be the greatest golfer ever, wrote the foreword to the book you now hold in your hands.

FOREWORD

Chi Chi Rodriguez: The man—the golfer—the humanitarian—the teacher—my friend! He is one of the finest human beings I have had the pleasure of knowing, and I am delighted to have the privilege of introducing you to Chi Chi's book, *101 Supershots.*

In the game of life, Chi Chi certainly has his priorities in order. His wife, Iwalani, and daughter, Donnette, come first—followed closely by the underprivileged children whom Chi Chi loves to teach about golf *and* life!

He has given so much of himself to so many that I consider him the game's finest ambassador of goodwill.

In the game of golf, Chi Chi has separated himself from the rest of the golf world with his uncanny knack for shotmaking.

Chi Chi is a genius at "supershots"—which he was forced to learn because of his boyhood practice with only a five-iron. He has so many shots in his bag that I could easily see the book from this master being titled "1,001 Supershots."

To illustrate Chi Chi's own unselfish nature, I want to share a story involving my oldest son, Jackie.

Jackie, who is a young professional golfer, wanted to improve his short game and came to me for advice. I immediately suggested that he go to see the master of the short game—Chi Chi.

Chi Chi and Iwalani took Jackie into their home —treated him like a son—and Chi Chi worked tirelessly with Jackie on the practice tee. When he returned home, Jackie had learned an impressive collection of shots and I, in turn, asked him to show them to me. (The use of Chi Chi's "supershots" actually helped me in my 1986 Masters victory.)

Thanks, Chi Chi, for what you mean to the game of golf and for what you mean to me and my family as a friend.

And a special thanks for sharing your *101 Supershots.*

JACK NICKLAUS

INTRODUCTION

Early on, while learning to play golf as a boy in Puerto Rico, I quickly realized that neither the swing nor the course the game is played on was ever meant to be mastered. After all, even a well-grooved, technically sound golf swing is extremely difficult (if not truly impossible) to repeat every time, owing to constant changes in a player's flexibility, mental attitude, strength, and natural timing and tempo. Another reason why golf can never be played totally to perfection is that on-course hazards bordering the straight and narrow path of the fairway and surrounding greens await off-line shots or a ball that takes an unlucky bad bounce. This is why you should be equipped with an arsenal of shots that allow you to save par when your tee shot fails to split the fairway or your approach fails to find the green.

The irony of my learning to play this great game of golf—initially with a guava stick for a club and a crushed-up tin can for a ball, and later with a "real" ball, but only a five-iron, is that it was an *advantage*, not a disadvantage, as one might naturally perceive it to be. Both of these rather rustic types of apprenticeship sharpened my hand-eye coordination and heightened my sense of touch or "feel" for hitting a particular distance.

But playing one club golf was mostly responsible for my educating myself to work the club precisely on different paths and planes, and also at varying speeds, because this is the only way you can improvise and hit a variety of shots with only a five-iron. For example, to play a 20-yard shot out of the rough to a pin tucked close behind a greenside bunker, I had to exaggeratedly open the clubface of the five-iron and swing very slowly on an upright out-to-in path so that I cut across the ball at impact, thereby imparting a small degree of cutspin on it, which is what enabled it to hold the green. Of course, once I was fortunate enough to own a complete set of "sticks," I chose a more lofted sand wedge to handle this lie and course situation, because this club features 56 degrees of loft (24 degrees more than a five-iron), which is a key ingredient for hitting a high, soft, quick-stopping greenside shot. What I found so amazing, once I had the luxury of holding a wedge in my hands, is that the basic principles I had adhered to while hitting the improvised short shot with a five-iron essentially remained the same with a wedge, thus making the execution of the shot easier. Now I could stick the ball close to the hole, not just get it to stay somewhere on the green.

I think you probably have guessed where I'm headed: My shotmaking prowess is a learned skill, an art. It is not inborn. Rather, I learned almost all 101 of the shots contained in this book by experimentation with different setups and swings, practicing hitting out of various types of lies, remaining patient and persevering when my game was sour.

Amigos, I think once you discover how much more pleasurable the game becomes when you can draw a tee-shot around a dogleg left hole, hit an imaginative approach shot over or under a tree and tight to the flagstick, blast the ball close to the hole from a buried lie in sand, sink a sharp-breaking putt—and much more—you'll be very willing to sacrifice some of your valuable playing time for practice time. I guarantee, the more you practice the art of shotmaking, the more it will feel less like work and more like fun, even while you grind away mentally. More important, developing a good shot-making repertoire will allow you to see the game in a whole different light. Instead of being angry about hitting the ball in trouble, you will welcome the challenge of recovering, simply because you are so fully prepared to tackle any lie.

Bear in mind, however, that the road to developing a host of shots will not always be bump free. At times, expect to feel frustration, especially when learning short finesse shots. They take longer to master because of the unique changes you must make in your normal setup and swing. Moreover, these types of greenside techniques are naturally more exacting because you are aiming for a smaller target area around the hole, not the relatively wide expanse of fairway as you would on a drive nor the fat of the green as you would for what could be called a "long" approach. Because, too, the importance of precision—good hand and wrist action—is a priority, as is a smooth-flowing, often syrupy swing tempo.

Preparation through steady practice is the only honest avenue to achieving your shotmaking potential. It may sound like a tough assignment, but it won't be if you practice methodically, working from the setup to the backswing to the downswing. When learning each shot, try to feel the key motions and be patient; it takes time for all the technical points to slip nicely, and one hopes permanently, into your muscle-memory. Don't worry, once you see results—how practicing and learning these shots can lower your handicap and make you enjoy the game more—you will not be afraid to work extra hard. Take it from Chi Chi, it will be well worth it!

101
SUPERSHOTS
••••••••••••••••••••••••••

ON THE TEE

The *tee*, a relatively small area of fine manicured grass bordered by two tiny markers and featuring a plate or sign marking the hole's yardage, is truly where the action begins eighteen times during a full round of golf. Hit a nicely struck tee-shot in the fairway (or to the green on a par-3) and right away you increase your percentages for shooting a par or birdie.

Solid, steady practice is obviously a prerequisite to consistently hitting the tee-ball, or *drive*, purely and pretty much exactly where you desire. Common sense and a clear-cut strategy are of great importance, too. You have to know when it's best to leave the driver in the bag and be disciplined enough to take out and hit either a one-iron or fairway wood instead. You must also know how to handle wind. Then, too, you must know how to work the ball around differently shaped dogleg holes. Also, on par-3s you have to know precisely what club to hit off the tee and when and how to spin the ball in order to land it close to the hole.

The true secrets, however, toward evolving into

a refined shot maker, who can produce again and again in a friendly match as well as in the heat of competitive pressure, are setting up correctly and comfortably to the ball and bringing your natural, even-flowing practice swing to the golf course.

When I reflect on my early days as a tour professional and analyze my former immature playing habits, I sometimes get downright angry. I can't tell you how many times I just walked up to the ball and quickly hit it without first planning a sound, score-conscious strategy, acquainting myself with a rhythmic swinging motion (via a rehearsal of a smooth practice swing), and aligning my body and the club to a distinct, distant target. In thinking about my old mistakes now, I guess I loved swinging extra fast so much that I didn't care if the ball landed in play. Regrettably, I paid dearly for the stupidity of treating the game of golf like a lottery. If I had stuck to a specific preswing regimen and concentrated hard on hitting the ball to a precise target in the fairway (either straight down the middle or to the left or right), I would have left myself the best possible angle for playing an approach shot onto the green. Consequently, I would have penciled in more birdies than bogies on my scorecard and thus won even more tournaments—and money!—on the PGA Tour.

Nowadays, I'm still a very speedy player, but I'm rarely sloppy about how I ready myself to tee off. Before hitting I make sure I'm fully prepared mentally and physically so that I can play the best possible shot. And that new careful *countdown* is a big reason why, in just a short time on the Senior PGA Tour, I've earned a far greater amount of money than I earned playing the regular PGA Tour for twenty-five years.

You, too, will raise the level of your game by becoming a smoother swinger, richer shotmaker, and lower scorer if you stick faithfully to an organized preswing countdown. So here are three vital routines to learn and put permanently into your repertoire.

LESSON ONE: *Take less time to read the scorecard and more time to read the hole. Think discretion, not distance.*

Going strictly by a hole's yardage is no way to decide whether or not to play a driver off the tee. The severity of trouble bordering the fairway should play the key role in your final choice of club and shot.

On a long and narrow hole, think twice about hitting a driver. When your swing's not quite sharp or your confidence level is low or you just feel a bit tentative, a one-iron or three-wood are more sensible choices of club, for both are easier to control than standard drivers. This switch may cause you to give up some distance, but not necessarily. And that small sacrifice may be worth it because you'll be hitting a second shot from short fairway grass rather than from trouble bordering the tight hole.

LESSON TWO: *Stare at your target (whether a small area of green near the flagstick on a par-3 or a wider area of fairway or a par-4 or par-5 hole), and then tell yourself: "That's where I'm going to hit the ball."*

When you look intensely at your target and clearly visualize the shape of the shot you want to play, you encourage your body to swing the club in a particular way, which will enable you to hit the desired shot.

If, on the other hand, you stand on the tee and shift your focus from the target to a hazard you fear, you'll make all kinds of unconscious compensations in your swing just to avoid hitting the ball there, and in doing this you'll hit the ball wildly into trouble on the other side of the fairway.

LESSON THREE: *Pretend that your practice swing is the real swing. Then, when it comes time to play your tee-shot, your technique won't be "make believe."*

A practice swing shouldn't serve solely to relax your muscles, but more as a way to rehearse the correct body movements involved in the back-and-through motions. Concentrating on slowly taking the club away, setting it securely at the top, and making an accelerating swish going through the ball should be your key objectives. If you fail to feel the swing you want on the first go, take a couple of deep breaths and relax into the right movements. Then you'll address the ball with confidence and concentrate more on swinging the club and less on hitting at the ball.

SHOT
1 THE POWER-DRAW

••

I'd be a liar if I called my swing orthodox. Although I stick to a particular set of fundamentals that govern grip, stance, aim, and alignment—as do all fine players—I'm more of a hard hitter of the ball than a smooth swinger of the golf club. Because of my physical limitations—being 5 feet 7½ inches tall and weighing 132 pounds—I can't swing as smoothly as, say, Gene Littler, whom I call the Fred Astaire of the Senior Tour. Boy, is he smooth. Me, I'm aggressive. I let the club rip!

I believe that although my swing is not of the

The power-draw is the shot all fine players hit on sharp dogleg left holes.

copybook style, it requires far less practice and is actually simpler to imitate than the typical classic method. Not only does it induce confidence, because I think of swinging "through" the ball instead of clogging my head with technical mumbo-jumbo, but it feels more natural. The biggest bonus of my swing, however, is that it allows me to hit the ball easily and powerfully in a right-to-left draw pattern. That shape of shot imparts overspin to the ball at contact and gives me increased yardage. This distance advantage of the power-draw shot makes it worth trying, particularly if your swing isn't producing the "big ball." Here's how I hit it.

In setting up to play the power-draw drive, I first tee the ball very *high* so that when it sits on the peg it is totally above the top of the club's face. This raised tee position promotes a flat arc of swing, which in turn allows my hands and forearms to *roll over* through impact. These rolling-over actions also make the clubface roll over at impact, which is basically how heavy right-to-left overspin is imparted on the ball.

Teeing up the ball extra high promotes the flat swing plane you desire when hitting a power-draw.

To further encourage a flatter swing plane, I strengthen my grip by turning both of my hands a hair clockwise, until the Vs formed by each thumb and forefinger point to my right shoulder as I set the driver behind the ball. The clubhead is soled in such a way that its face is looking well right of target, to allow for the draw-shape of shot.

To promote a very active and free and natural turn of my right hip on the backswing (in order to make room for the club to swing on a flatter plane), I set my right foot back a couple inches from the normal, "square" position.

Since I will want to extend the club back *low and inside* the target line in the takeaway (to promote a powerful arc on the backswing), I assume a wide stance. Standing with your feet too close together causes you to pick up the club too quickly in the takeaway, which narrows your swing arc and thus ultimately cuts off power.

To maximize the width of my backswing *arc*, I start moving my whole body laterally off the ball to the right—away from the target—as soon as I trigger the takeaway. This highly unorthodox key increases the distance the clubhead travels and thereby gives me the length of swing arc of a much taller man. Using this method, I'm able to hit the ball much farther down the fairway than I would if I employed the standard, copybook swing.

Going back, I bend my knees deeper and rotate them and my hips more vigorously than the typical professional, which puts me into a semicrouched position at the top. Although this action isn't one of the prettiest on the Senior Tour, my fellow pros tell me it is one of the most rhythmic and repeatable. When my left knee points several inches behind the ball and I feel lively tension in my left hip, I know I'm wound up, ready to whack the ball.

Once I reach the top, I uncoil, or "fire," my right

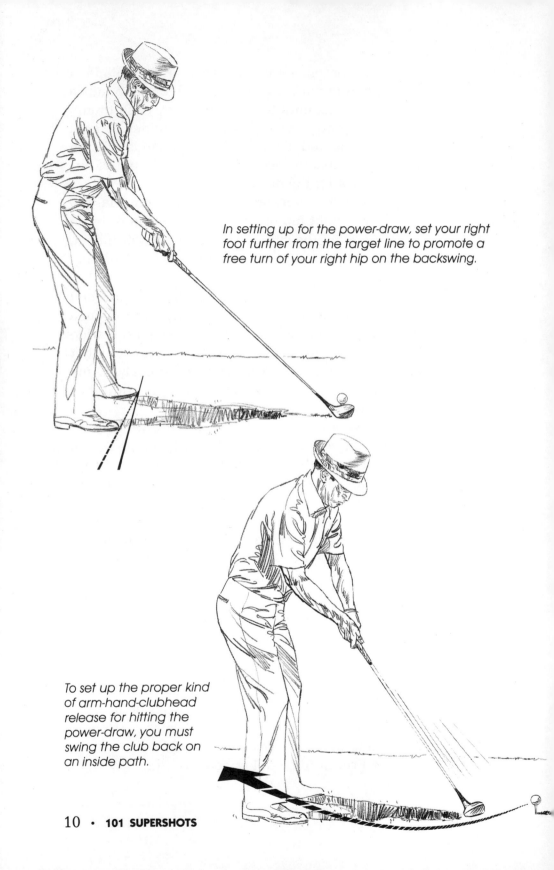

In setting up for the power-draw, set your right foot further from the target line to promote a free turn of your right hip on the backswing.

To set up the proper kind of arm-hand-clubhead release for hitting the power-draw, you must swing the club back on an inside path.

As soon as the power-draw downswing is triggered, you should feel a pulse of power being transmitted through your arms and hands to the clubhead.

When hitting the power-draw, the perfectly timed unraveling of your lower body increases the whipping power of the club through impact.

hip, which pushes my weight back over to my left side and swivels my knees toward the target. Both of those movements help me regain my balance and truly ready me for the hit. Releasing my right side powerfully toward the target also helps me clear my left hip more quickly and easily. Once that clearing action is triggered, my arms extend out at the ball. At this point in the swing, it's almost as if I can feel the building pulse of power being transmitted through my arms and hands. When my hands drop to a level even with my thighs, I start rotating my right forearm in a counterclockwise direction. The instant this rotation begins, multiplying power starts being *transferred* down the clubshaft into the clubhead. Then, once I release my hands with the final, delayed uncocking of the wrists, the clubhead is whipped into the ball while it's starting to close, thereby creating draw-flight and the powerful overspin I need to pass the big guys.

S H O T

2 THE POWER-FADE

The ability to curve a golf ball in the air from left to right is an advantage on courses that feature par-4 holes that bend to the right, starting at a point around 175 yards off the tee. Once you learn how to play the power-fade, you'll be able to wind the ball around these dogleg holes, setting up shorter approach shots onto the greens. That's how you'll save vital shots. The player who can't play a power-fade will often leave himself a much longer, tougher second shot, usually with a wood or long iron. I think you probably know those less-lofted clubs are much harder to hit and control than the short and medium irons. But, enough of a pep talk, here are my keys for playing the power-fade tee-shot.

From the time I pull the driver out of my bag, I prepare both mentally and physically for playing a very different shape of shot. Before setting up, instead of visualizing a draw pattern in my mind's eye, I see the ball sliding from left to right in the air. Then, once I'm actually standing to the ball—which is teed up *extra low* to promote an upright swing—I start rehearsing the key physical motions I want and need to employ. I'll explain those in detail, but first let's take a much closer look at the setup, since the way I address the ball determines how I swing.

I set up to the low-teed ball with sound posture—knees flexed slightly, back relatively straight, and arms hanging quite naturally from the shoulders. I do not, however, set my body square to my final

Teeing the ball low promotes the upright swing plane you desire for hitting a power-fade.

landing target. Rather, I aim the clubface at a spot well left of my final target and set my shoulders and feet parallel to an imaginary line running from the ball to that spot. This spot, left of your final target, is what you should swing away from on the backswing and then toward on the downswing. With the clubface open at the precise moment of impact, the ball starts flying to that spot along the line of your swing path, then drifts back to your final target. To promote the proper clubface position at impact, I grip the club more firmly than normal with the last three fingers of my left hand.

In starting the club back, I swing along a line parallel to my open shoulders. *Low and slow* are the buzzwords I use during the takeaway, because a controlled dragging of the clubhead promotes a coordinated turning motion of my shoulders and hips. I know if I get too quick in the takeaway, I'll yank the club up, on too steep an angle, with my hands. When I do that I fail to shift my weight to my right side on the backswing and don't coil my hips and shoulders as tightly as I should, thus I am robbed of power at impact. So I must feel that the clubshaft is an extension of my left arm and shoulder, then swing the unit slowly back as if it were one piece.

I continue swinging the club back to thigh height with my wrists still uncocked. Here my right arm folds naturally, as if I were starting to make an underhanded throw. Ultimately, this folding action is necessary for me to make an upswing hit of club-on-ball at the moment of truth—impact. The good news is that this folding of the right arm will occur all by itself if, and only if, my takeaway "hook" remains: *Swing the left arm and clubshaft back together.*

Maintaining a one-piece left-sided takeaway also

helps you keep the left wrist firm and flat (the back of it is in line with the left forearm), which keeps the clubface square to your spot. Attempting to employ the one-piece move with your right hand and arm could cause your right elbow to fly away from your body on the backswing. This is a technical hindrance because it steepens the swing drastically and automatically turns the clubface into a faulty position. (Until you memorize the proper one-piece takeaway motion, monitor the position of the swinging clubhead. As your hands reach thigh height and the clubhead reaches the level of your knees, the toe of the club should point skyward.

Once I feel most of my weight flow into my right foot and drop my right leg, I cock my wrists and swing up to the three-quarter position, all the time maintaining the in-line position of the left wrist and left forearm. You must do the same, because it is this position that keeps the left hand in control of the swing.

Although my swing is very short, I'm in a very powerful position once I reach the three-quarter point. That's because I tighten my upper body spring to the maximum by turning into a braced right leg.

The second half of the swing must be triggered by the lower body. More precisely, my left leg is the first to move as it bows out to the left. This one move triggers a strong pulling action through my entire left side.

You'll know if you're starting down correctly if you feel a tug on your left hip, as the arms, hands, and club descend together. To ensure the vital late hit, it's critical to wait to feel this tug before you release your right side. Otherwise, you'll never retain the control angle that the left arm made with the clubshaft at the top of your swing.

One big backswing key for hitting a controlled power-fade is making a very compact upright swinging action.

Holding back the release of the left forearm-wrist-hand unit is the most important downswing key for hitting a power-fade.

If the right shoulder thrusts violently outward at the start of the downswing—the number-one fault made by Mr. Average—you'll throw the arc of the swing outside the proper swing path and never hit the shot you planned to play. Normally, you'll hit a weak slice instead of a power-fade. However, if the right hand violently takes over, you'll roll the clubface over in the hit zone and thus pull the ball well left of target. (I realize power comes from the right hand, nevertheless never think too hard about working it. The right hand will correctly come into play when the hands drop to hip height in the downswing—if the left hand has been previously fully in command.)

As the clubhead approaches the ball, my left hip starts to turn left, or "clear," which opens up a passageway for my swinging arms. Then, as my legs drive, my upper body and head stay behind the ball. All the time this is going on, I'm gripping more firmly with my left hand and pulling the clubface powerfully into the back of the ball. Make sure you, too, squeeze the handle and delay the release of your left forearm-wrist-hand, otherwise your right hand will faultily take over, causing a mishit.

TAILORING THE TIP

To help you hit the power-fade, here's a trick I learned from my friend Lee Trevino.

After you set up, imagine that there are three golf balls teed up in front of the one you're about to hit. For the power-fade, you want to hit through all four balls. This will force your right shoulder down rather than around, on the downswing, with your arms extending toward the target on the follow-through. As a result, you hold your release, keep the club moving down the line, and fade the ball to its destination.

3 THE ONE-IRON DRIVE

The ability to hit a one-iron straight down the center of the fairway is a particular advantage on short, narrow par-5 holes, when precision is the priority. Nevertheless, to master the one-iron drive you must be willing to develop a new attitude and to work new responses into your muscle-memory.

The club-level player, who has yet to learn how to hit a one-iron proficiently, frequently puts himself behind the eight ball on narrow holes by playing a driver and hitting a wild shot. Or he hits the ball so far down the fairway on a short par-4 hole that he faces a very difficult finesse wedge shot, instead of an easier, full short iron, which a one-iron off the tee would have left him.

To be an expert one-iron player, you must fine-tune your confidence level by washing all negative thoughts from your brain. Frankly, a positive attitude is more important on this shot than maybe on any other, because the one-iron is the toughest iron in the bag to hit solidly into the air. Therefore, before setting up to play a shot, see yourself making a strong windup, then unleashing your power, and finally, hitting the ball into the perfect position on the fairway from which to play an approach to the flagstick.

Your other vital keys are physical. Before readying yourself to hit, wiggle your feet until you feel a lively springiness, or bounce, in your legs. Then cock your head to the right so that you feel it's behind the ball. Finally, hold the club lightly in the fingers of your right hand. All of these keys, plus teeing up the ball, induce such strong feelings of physical power that your level of confidence will reach its highest possible peak before you even play the shot.

Since the purpose of playing this club is to hit the ball with pinpoint accuracy, put yourself in the ultimate control position by standing with your feet perfectly square to the target. In other words, a straight line drawn across the toes of each shoe would run parallel to the target line. Be sure, however, that the toe end of your right shoe is perpendicular to the target-line; that foot position will help you wind powerfully into your right side on the backswing, with no sway of the body. Your left foot should be fanned out slightly to your left, about 30 degrees, since this position allows you to clear your left hip powerfully on the downswing.

The backswing needs only to be smooth, because the long shaft of the one-iron makes it simpler to generate more than sufficient clubhead speed. Don't lose this built-in advantage by making a short, quick action. Swing back nice and long, maintaining a good rhythm and tempo.

The downswing you employ should be closer to the *sweep* you use with your woods, than the sharper, more abrupt downward hit with your short irons.

TAILORING THE TIP

Should the fairways be wet, simply widen the arc of your backswing, since this ultimately allows you to hit a more powerful shot that flies longer in the air. To do this, keep your wrists locked and extend the club back to about waist level, as if you were trying to put the one-iron's clubhead in a baseball glove being worn by a friend. Then swing up to the top, turning your shoulders and hips powerfully, and boosting your hands higher over your head than normal.

4 THE WIND TAMER

One of the most problematic shots for the average golfer is the tee-shot into a strong headwind. The basic reason for this is that the typical amateur can't accept the wind as part of the game. He worries so much about losing distance that he figures the only way to make up lost ground is to swing very fast. This is a big mistake, and it's one I learned early not to make.

As a boy, while caddying in Puerto Rico where the winds often truly howl, I watched the drives of local amateurs "balloon," or rise too high into the air, because they swung too hard. What you must realize is that the harder you swing, the more backspin is put on the ball. Furthermore, the action of the wind puts even more backspin on the ball.

Next time you're out on the course playing golf on a windy day, make a slower backswing than you do normally. That way you'll make a full release of your hands on the downswing and impart less backspin on the ball, too. The shots you hit will bore into the wind like bullets shot out of a rifle.

Before concerning yourself with swing tempo, however, check your setup, because things like tee height and ball position also affect the shot's trajectory. Playing the ball back slightly in your stance and teeing it slightly lower than normal is standard good advice for cheating a strong wind, provided it's not overdone. If you make the errors of playing the ball close to your right foot and teeing it so low that it's practically level with the grass, you'll hit down on it, causing it to fly too high in the wind.

Unless the wind is very strong, I think there's a lot to be said for simply teeing the ball at the normal height and in its regular position in relation to your stance. If you do that, and swing slowly, you may discover it's the only adjustment you need to make.

Straightening your right arm, releasing your hands fully, and driving the clubhead targetward are three critical keys to hitting a tee-shot that tames the wind.

5 THE WIND RIDER

A downwind drive is a favorite shot of the average golfer. Nevertheless, often a mishit results because the player gets overconfident and tries to hit the ball a country mile. It's true that a favoring wind will send your ball flying farther down the fairway, but only if you meet it solidly at impact with the sweet spot of the driver-face.

Apart from swinging too hard, the typical amateur fails to hit a good shot when the wind's behind his back because he plays the ball too far forward in his stance. Playing a tee-shot opposite your left toe will lead to a "top." You should, however, tee the ball slightly forward of the normal left-heel position, simply because playing it in that spot sets you up more behind the ball than usual.

When you're hitting a downwind drive you will often feel as if the wind could actually be powerful enough to push you toward the target too soon in the downswing. Because you fear this, your tendency is to rush the swing in an attempt to hit in between gusts. Because quickening your tempo will affect your technique and shot negatively, stay-behind-the-ball should be your mental key when addressing a downwind tee-shot.

TAILORING THE TIP

Those players who have difficulty hitting a driver well should switch to a three-wood when a healthy wind is with them. This club is more lofted, thus it will send the ball up in the tailwind more quickly and send it zooming down the fairway.

SHOT
6 THE FIVE-WOOD WINNER

A common sight on any golf course is a player trying to slug a two-iron on a long par-3 hole and missing the green by a long way. This, to me, is a stupid strategy. Don't try to be a macho man. If your heart tells you to force a long iron, but your head tells you not to because you lack consistency with the less lofted clubs, listen to your intellect.

As that old golf saying goes, "Swing the force, don't force the swing." And a better force for the average player to swing on a 175-to-200-yard par-3 is a five-wood.

The five-wood is a more sole-weighted club than a two-iron, thus it is much simpler to hit in the air and control. Also, you'll feel more confident hitting a five-wood. Furthermore, the five-wood is considerably longer and heavier than a two-iron, therefore you'll put more power behind the ball at impact.

I hope I've convinced many of you medium-high handicappers to turn in your two-iron for a five-wood. If so, read this tip for playing it off a tee on a long par-3 hole.

Tee up so that when you sole the club behind the ball it is slightly above the top of the clubface. This will encourage making a sweep more than a hit.

At address, my stance is a hair closed, with my right foot pulled back about an inch or two from my left. I stand closed because I like a touch of right-to-left movement on most of my shots. You, however, would be better off standing square—aiming feet, knees, hips, and shoulders parallel to the target line—since that will best allow you to swing the club on the correct, inside-square-inside path. Keep the clubface square to your target, too, when addressing the ball, which should be played off your left heel.

Good *balance* is also paramount for hitting solid five-wood shots, so distribute your weight evenly between the ball and heel of each foot.

I could write an entire book on the intricacies of my swing for hitting a five-wood, but I'm not going to do that here for fear of confusing you. Since I'm covering all kinds of shots, I will cite, instead, my most critical swing keys. Learn them through steady practice and the rest of the puzzle pieces will fit together.

Because I'm trying to hit a small target, pinpoint accuracy is more of a priority than power. Therefore, I shorten the takeaway some and swing up sooner, making less of a body turn than I normally do on drives. I do, nevertheless, swing the club back very deliberately to trigger a smooth tempo.

I swing back only to the three-quarter position because a short swing almost always works best for me. Test for your own perfect length of swing by varying it in practice.

It's the return to my left side that sparks my downswing. Personally, thrusting my legs helps me get over to my left side. You may find it works best to replant your left heel or clear your left hip. Experiment to determine which physical technique suits you.

As soon as my weight shifts to the inside of my left foot, my arm-hand unit falls almost straight down. Then, as weight transfers to the outside portion of that same foot, I pull the club down, and whip it through the ball at a speed of about 120 mph. Through impact, all I feel I do is focus my eyes on the back of the ball and hold on to the handle, while my left hand leads and my right hand provides the power.

With practice, this shot can be easily perfected. Moreover, it will save you vital strokes on long par-3 holes. So go to work.

S·H·O·T

7 THE QUICK-STOPPER

I love to hit a shot that has so much backspin it practically stops on a dime.

If you're like most amateurs, you probably think these shots hit stiff to the flag are beautiful to watch, too. However, you might believe, deep down, that only a pro like me can play one. That's not so; you can learn to play a "stopper" yourself. But before I go into how to put backspin on the ball, let me tell you some facts about it.

What is *backspin*? Backspin, or the upward roll of the ball on the clubface at impact, provides the lift force needed to keep the ball in the air and gets it to do a dance on the green.

To impart maximum backspin on the ball, you must strike it without making any contact with the ground behind it. If sand gets between the ball and the clubface spin is reduced, causing the ball to fly 10 to 20 yards farther than normal and land with no bite.

The divot that flies in the air when I hit either a quick-stopping short or medium iron shot has nothing to do with imparting backspin on the ball. Shaving a divot of turf on iron shots is inevitable, because of the way I come sharply into the ball.

In several situations on par-3 holes—most notably, when the pin is cut behind a bunker on the green's bottom tier—I'll need to impart backspin on the ball if I want it to finish in birdie range. The accompanying schematic shows a situation in which backspin is a bonus. An iron shot overshooting the pin could bounce over the green and leave a treacherous downhill putt.

To hit a high-flying, biting iron shot, tee up so that the sweet spot of the clubface is even with the back portion of the ball. Golfers who don't take advantage of being permitted to tee the ball up for their first shot on a hole are silly. Hitting off the turf could very easily cause the ball to "fly," due to dirt or moist blades of grass intervening at impact.

The most critical feature of the address is ball position. You must play the ball back in your stance because a rearward placement promotes a steep backswing and descending blow.

I suggest you employ a more controlled three-quarter swing, especially since on most par-3 holes you're hitting only a short or medium iron club into the green. A big windup of your body and a lengthy swing are not at all necessary.

Your swing hook on the downswing should always be to keep your hands ahead of the clubhead, for that will help you pull the clubface into the back of the ball, and hit with a nice clean nipping action.

TAILORING THE TIP

If the green you're hitting to is baked out and the pin placement is tight, try swinging from out to in, to impart a soft degree of cutspin on the ball.

In hitting a quick-stopping iron shot, key on keeping your hands leading the clubhead on the downswing.

CHI CHI'S CLINIC

WARM-UP TIME

Rushing to the first tee without warming up is foolish. You should always lubricate your golf muscles by hitting a few practice shots with a variety of clubs. Begin with small swings with a short iron, then slowly work your way to a driver. If you lack the time to hit balls before you play, swing a weighted club or two irons back and forth in slow motion. Either of these preround workouts will help you loosen up and slow your rhythm.

ANTIDOTES FOR FIRST-TEE JITTERS

The first tee of a golf course is where the typical club-level player often hits his poorest shots of the day. The reason: nerves! The cause of the player's tension: fear of mishitting the shot or in some cases missing the ball completely in front of his playing partners or fellow members.

When it comes time for you to play your opening tee-shot, take a couple of deep breaths to relax and see a movie of a perfect shot play in your mind as you prepare to hit. Then swing at only 75 percent of your maximum power.

Concentrating hard on the shot at hand will take your mind off the gallery of your buddies milling around the first tee. The real bonus, however, will come from your tension-free, compact swing; you'll be surprised how far and straight you'll hit the ball by limiting yourself to three-quarters of your power.

AIM AWAY FROM TROUBLE

Get in the habit of teeing up on the trouble side of the tee when preparing to hit a tee-shot. Aiming away from dense trees, out of bounds, water, and so on, will boost your confidence because your chances of hitting the safe open space of the fairway are increased. Moreover, when you're confident, you make a free, uninhibited swing.

NEW CLUBS CAN HELP

Many senior golfers hit weak tee-shots because they stick to equipment that no longer fits them. If you're falling short of your "old" landing spots in the fairway, try lighter-model clubs with flexible shafts that are easier to swing. Also, ask your pro to change your grips for thinner ones, so that you can release your hands freely in the hitting area.

THE NAME GAME

In teeing up, always make sure the brand name of the ball is visible. Moreover, set it on the peg so that when you look down it's running horizontally along the target line. This systematic method of teeing, in addition to helping you align the sweet spot of the clubface square to the target, encourages you to keep your eyes intensely focused on the ball until the club makes it disappear at impact. Consequently, you'll hit many more solid, accurate shots.

HOW TO BUY DISTANCE

Short players are sometimes hampered by a narrow arc of swing that causes them to lose vital distance off the tee.

Those of you who are short like me, and don't have the time to revamp your technique totally on the practice tee, can "buy" arc—and driving distance—by purchasing a longer than standard club from your local golf professional. Because the longer club increases the radius of your left arm and the clubshaft, your swing arc widens, and you can generate more power.

HOW TO REHEARSE BODY COIL

Those of you who hit weak drives should learn how to wind up your body correctly, like a coiled spring, by doing the following exercise:

Stand as if you're ready to hit, but with a club behind your back, hooked through your arms. Now, instead of raising up and weakening your turning action, rotate your upper body fully to the right, on a horizontal plane.

This drill, in addition to imparting the right turning movement into your muscle-memory, will serve as a great preround warm-up exercise.

CURE FOR "CASTING"

Releasing the hands too early at the start of the downswing ("casting") is one of the most often-repeated faults of the average golfer and a direct cause of sliced drives. This technical bug can usually be traced to an overly long swing, which causes one's wrists to get into a flimsy position at the top, when the club drops well below the parallel position.

To cure the swing problem and, with it your slice, imagine the driver you're swinging is a medium iron.

Now, you'll automatically make a controlled, compact swing and arrive at a more secure position at the top. From there you can swing nicely through the ball.

BALANCE DRILLS

Balance is the most underrated element of the golf swing because it affects tempo, timing, and rhythm. If your balance is good, the swing flows and a solid hit feels effortless.

To enhance your balance, hit a few practice shots with your feet together. Then graduate to standing on your left leg only and hitting long, medium, and short iron shots off a tee.

Return to your normal stance after hitting a small bucket of balls off one leg and you'll be itching to "eat" up those par-3 holes.

2

ON THE FAIRWAY

Hearing amateur golfers talking among themselves at the nineteenth hole after a round never fails to strike my funny bone. That's because they usually talk about what they should have done out on the course. Ironically, they "cry" about hitting a wild tee-shot, playing a bad chip, or missing a putt. For some reason, however, they rarely talk about playing a poor approach shot onto a green. This truly surprises me. I guess the reason they neglect talking about this element of the game is that, in the typical club-level player's mind, hitting an approach shot with an iron or wood club is less of an art than smashing a tee-shot straight down the middle of the fairway or sinking a long breaking putt.

Although there is some truth to that way of thinking, hitting an approach is no piece of cake, just because the shot is being played off manicured fairway grass. To hit the ball close to the hole, you not only have to calculate the distance of the shot and choose the correct club, but you also have to know how to deal with varying wind conditions and wet grass, and be smart enough to predict how far the ball is going to bounce forward or spin back once it lands on the green. You also have to swing with your usual rhythm and tempo so that you hit a particular club your usual distance. But, most of all, you must align your body and the club perfectly according to the shape of shot you're trying to hit. As Jack Nicklaus once said to me: "Chi Chi, if you address the ball correctly, there's a good chance you'll hit a decent approach shot, even if you make a mediocre swing. If you set up incorrectly, you'll hit a poor shot, even if you make the best swing in the world."

I've always thought that aligning myself to a target was very similar to aiming a gun. To fire a rifle at a target, you set your body in a way that permits you to aim the gun's barrel directly and precisely at the target's bull's-eye. The same basic principle applies in golf. Unless you are setting up to play one of my fancy shots, you should align your feet, knees, hips, and shoulders parallel to the target line —or "square" to it. The clubface should be pointing directly at your target.

Learning to aim correctly is the foundation of hitting pinpoint approach shots. So, if your desire is to be a dead-eye-Dick type of shotmaker, incorporate these alignment keys into the routine you use when playing an approach shot.

Start your routine by standing a few feet behind the ball and staring very intently at the flag or a small area of green around it. I find the more tuned in I am to my target, the more confident I become. That positiveness, in turn, seems to ease any body tension or general stiffness I might be experiencing, thereby ultimately allowing my swing to become one uninterrupted flowing motion.

Next, feel the club in your hands and wait for that feeling to intensify as you mentally see yourself setting up, swinging the club rhythmically, and hitting a finely executed shot.

Now, stand to the ball, assuming a setup that's right for the swing you visualized in your mind's eye and physically practiced.

Once you've moved your feet into a square position, be sure that your shoulders are square, too, unless you are trying to shape a shot. Misaligned shoulders prevent you from correctly swinging on the normally desired inside-square-inside path.

When you feel comfortably correct, sole the club behind the ball, squarely to your target. To check that the clubface is correctly square, imagine a path (formed by the two vertical lines enclosing the scoring lines on a conventional clubface) running straight down the target line. In aligning wood shots, use the top edge of the face to help you.

Next, look back and forth a few times, staring at the target, then the ball, until you feel yourself getting into a concentrative mental cocoon. Then, waggle the club and swing.

SHOT

8 THE OFF-THE-DECK DRIVE

This is a "hero" shot that I play only when I absolutely have to. I'll hit it, either on a par-4 hole when the wind is blowing so strongly in my face that even a solid three-wood won't get the ball home or on a long par-5 hole that I must reach in two strokes, to set up an eagle or birdie that would put me back in contention to win a tournament.

Frankly, this is one of those shots you probably will not hit absolutely flush, unless the ball is sitting up nicely on fairway grass; at least half the ball

To smash a driver shot off fairway grass, hit against a firm left side.

should be above the top of the clubface. And of course a noncrackable state of confidence is also paramount, as is hitting against a firm left side.

In preparing to play this shot, you senior golfers

(who may be less flexible and have some trouble clearing your hips at the start of the downswing) should set up "open." That position will essentially put you in a preset clearance position. Just be cautious that you don't aim too far left of the target, which could cause you to mishit this shot.

You loose-as-a-goose players should set up square—with your feet, knees, hips, and shoulders parallel to the target line.

Whichever of those two setups you assume, play the ball forward in your stance, as that placement will best enable you to catch the ball solidly on the upswing.

In order to create power via a wide swing arc, *drag* the club straight back along the target line, well past your right foot. Then, swing upward, being sure to turn your upper body and raise your left heel off the ground. Both of those movements will boost your hands higher over your head, further widening the arc of your swing.

Don't rush the downswing or try lifting the ball by sort of pecking at it with the clubhead. The driver—especially in the modern-day metal designs that are heavily sole weighted—has plenty of loft to lift an propel the ball down the fairway. As good as the club is for the job, you still must focus on hitting against a firm left side; so trigger the second half of the swing by firing your right side first.

SHOT
9 THE POWER-SKY

On seaside courses, the wind tends to harden the greens. Therefore, from around 200 yards out in the fairway, a high four-wood shot is usually a smarter play than hitting a low-boring long iron that runs on after landing.

To hit the power-sky, I stand quite near the ball at address to encourage an upright swing angle and to take full advantage of the club's 19 degrees of loft at impact. Furthermore, I distribute my weight back on the heels of both feet to help me keep my body behind the ball. Don't ever make the error of putting too much weight on your toes, otherwise you'll cut drastically across the ball and hit a big slice.

On the backswing, I swing the club back low to the ground for only a few inches. Then quickly I set, or cock, my wrists to further ensure an *upright arc* of swing.

It's critical that the club move into the ball more at a downward angle than it does on a tee-shot; therefore, don't use as much leg action. (Trigger the downswing with a big lateral slide, and you'll create a shallow downswing arc.) Instead, clear your left hip speedily, so that weight shifts back to that side. Once that shift is triggered, pull the club down into the ball with your hands and arms.

SHOT
10 THE SIDESWIPE

Even the most level-looking fairway is rarely perfectly flat at any one spot. There are often depressions in the grass, some of which are much deeper than others.

Imagine that your ball lies in one of these spots, 180 yards from the green. Although the depression is pretty shallow, it still prevents you from sweeping the shot. What you must do then, to avoid hitting level ground behind the ball and coming up far short of your target, is take a four-wood and attack from a side angle.

The advantage of a four-wood over a two-iron is that even if you do come into the ball from too steep a plane, the club's loft will save the shot.

In setting up to play, address the ball so that it is closer to the neck of the club. This unorthodox position, plus standing open will encourage you to swing back outside the target line.

Keep the backswing action *short* for control.

Coming down, concentrate on holding the club's handle more tightly with your left hand.

Because you came into the ball from the right side (from outside the target line) and delayed the release by holding on with your left hand, the shot will start left and drift back to the target. Remember, then, to allow for the new flight.

SHOT 11 THE RUNNING LONG IRON

On an extremely narrow par-5 hole, with dense trees all the way down both sides of the fairway, a second shot with a three- or four-wood can be a risky gamble even for a low handicapper, especially if a swirling wind is liable to blow a high-hit ball into the boondocks. In such situations I often rely on a two- or three-iron, because either of these low-lofted clubs allows me to hit a dartlike shot that draws a bit in the air and runs fast upon landing. I actually pick up yardage going with an iron instead of a wood and hit a more accurate shot to boot.

Shifting your weight freely and fully to your left foot on the downswing is an important technical hook for hitting a running long iron.

To hit a low running shot, I set up with the ball midway between my feet and close my stance slightly by dropping my right foot back a couple of inches from my left. This slightly closed stance allows me to swing the club on an exaggerated inside path, which in turn causes my right hand to roll a little more quickly over my left hand through impact. When that happens, the clubface turns over, too, imparting a light drawspin on the ball.

Although the setup largely determines the type of swing motion you put on the ball, it's still highly important that you rotate both hips in a clockwise direction on the backswing, while feeling you are *turning in a barrel.* This powerful turning action will further promote a flat plane of swing and also enable you to wind like a tight-coiling spring. That coiling action will prove to be extremely beneficial on the downswing.

To spark the downward motion, rotate your left knee toward the target, then let the right knee follow. Once the hips snap back and the left one clears, your arms and hands will be driven downward, picking up speed as more of your weight shifts to your left side. As the clubface approaches the ball (swinging from a path inside the target line), your right forearm will roll over. Don't fight this by gripping tightly with your left hand. It's the one move that truly ensures your right hand and the clubface turn over simultaneously in the hit zone. If you just stay down and swing fully through the ball, you'll like the result. When hit right, this shot is truly a thing of beauty.

12 THE FINESSED LONG IRON

Long iron shots that fly high and stop quickly on a green are beautiful to watch and a definite scoring asset, thus every golfer's fantasy.

Two keys to playing this shot well are staying behind the ball through impact and contacting it on the upswing. Encourage these things to happen by playing the ball off your left instep, rather than your left heel.

On the backswing, simultaneously turn your hips and shoulders, then hinge your wrists as soon as you feel weight first shift over to the inside of your right foot. Soon into the takeaway, the back of your left hand should be flat and parallel to the target line—in the exact same position it should arrive at when you reach the top of your swing. Swing fully back on an upright plane and feel your weight slide fully into your braced right leg.

Start the downswing by moving your hips laterally. As weight transfers back to your left side and your arms whip down, resist the temptation to move your head. Once the club reaches hip level you want your right hand to release *under* your left. The upright plane of swing you created on the backswing, together with keeping your head behind the ball, will help you achieve that goal and produce that beautifully high long iron you dream about.

Remember: Set the wrists quickly on the backswing. Keep your head behind the ball and release your right hand under your left on the downswing.

13 THE BALL-ABOVE-YOUR-FEET BRUSH

This particular sloping lie makes you automatically swing the golf club on a flatter arc, which produces a right-to-left flying shot. Start, then, by making amends for this flight pattern by aiming your body and also the clubface to the right of the target you're hitting to—more if the slope's severe.

You'll get a better sense of feeling in control of the shot if you choke down on the club a couple of inches, since this brings you *closer* to the ball. You'll get a better sense of balance by setting most of your body weight toward your toes.

Swing compactly and smoothly going back.

Maintain your body level, or height, on the downswing—don't dip—since this encourages a nice sweeping action of club through ball.

The ball will tend to hook and roll farther, so take at least one less club, depending on the type of sidehill slope from which you're hitting.

TAILORING THE TIP

To handle this lie another way, set up square to your target, open the clubface (more, if the slope is severe), then make a normal swing.

The ball will fly pretty straight because opening the clubface compensates for the flatter swing you naturally make when hitting off this kind of slope. The club will thus return essentially to a square impact position. For this reason, select the same club you would hit normally from a designated distance.

14 THE BALL-BELOW-YOUR-FEET ATTACKER

When the lie of the ball is below your feet it's hard to stay down. Unless the slope of the land is very shallow and you can easily maintain your knee flex, the clubface will almost always be slightly open when contact is made, causing the ball to fade off to the right. Therefore, I suggest you allow for this pretty much inevitable shot pattern by pointing your body and the clubface to the left of your target.

During the motion, it's easy to fall forward, down a steep slope, so minimize this tendency by holding the club at its very end. To further preserve your balance, set more of your weight on the heels of your feet.

Swing the club back smoothly. Learn to accept the restricted length of the backswing that the lie dictates. Forcing a big turn only will lead to loss of balance and ultimately a poorly struck, wild shot.

On the downswing, transfer your weight back to your left foot. Grip more tightly with your left hand to prevent your right hand from rolling the club into such a closed position that you hit a violent hook.

TAILORING THE TIP

Here's another way of handling this slope. Align yourself parallel to an imaginary line that runs directly from the ball to your target. Next, close the clubface more or less, depending on how severely the land falls away from you. If the angle is sharp, close it more.

Then employ a slightly shorter, rhythmic swing. You'll see the ball will fly almost dead at your target.

SHOT
15 THE WIND-BATTLING DRAW

· ·

In a strong left-to-right crosswind, the percentage play is a draw. This shot will fly over the flag, hit the wall of wind blowing from the left, and fall softly to the green. Here's how to play it.

Address: Choke down on the handle a little bit to gain control of the club and thus control of the shot. Grip extra lightly to encourage a full release of your right hand over your left in the hitting area. Aim a hair to the right of the flagstick to allow for the draw flight of the ball. Be careful to play the ball back from its normal position or the clubface will be looking too far left at impact. If that happens, you'll hit a low pull that runs through the green.

Swing the club well inside the target line going back. Feeling your wrists and forearms rolling over, and sensing a vigorous hip turn, confirms that your backswing path of swing was sufficiently flat enough.

On the downswing, if you uncoil your left hip to the left and then turn your right forearm over in a counterclockwise direction, the blade will turn over through impact, causing the ball to draw into the powerful left-to-right crosswind.

16 THE WIND-BATTLING FADE

To be a true golfer, you must know how to deal with all kinds of weather conditions on the course, one of the hardest of which is a crosswind blowing from right to left.

Some players believe simply in aiming to the side from which the wind is blowing—the right—and letting the ball float back to the target. This sounds like a better strategy than it actually is, with its weak point being that it's very easy to hit the ball low under the wind. Therefore, your approach never blows back to your target. Instead of putting for birdie, you're in a trouble spot several yards to the side of the green.

Through experimenting in practice, I learned that the percentage shot in a strong right-to-left wind is a fade. This is a safe shot because by aiming to the left of the flag, you'll often hit the ball close to the stick and rarely miss the green. Think about it, even if your aiming and shot-making precision are so off that the ball fades too much, at worst the wind will probably blow it back to the light fringe where it's relatively easy for you still to save par with a good chip and one putt.

The most critical element of the setup is to stand open to the target. Aligning your body left of the target encourages you to swing along a path outside the target line on the backswing. That backswing path will cause you to swing across the line on the downswing. By cutting across the ball you impart left-to-right fade-spin on the ball.

The sensation that you're swinging the club far away from your body on the backswing confirms that it's moving outside the target line. This is unorthodox but correct for hitting this shot.

Drive your hips laterally at the start of the downswing and squeeze the grip firmly with the last three fingers of your left hand as you pull the club down into the ball. This will discourage an overactive premature release of the hands that would lead to a badly hooked shot.

The ball will fly off the clubface, fade in the air, and fall softly to the green.

SHOT

17 THE SWEEPER

On almost all southern courses in the United States, particularly in Florida, the grass in the fairways is of a coarse type called *Bermuda*.

The ball sits up very nicely on Bermuda grass, rarely snuggling itself among the blades, as it does on the bent grass fairways of the northern states. This makes iron play a true pleasure, provided you employ the correct swing technique.

If you plan a golf trip to Florida, the Carolinas, Bermuda, or the Caribbean, learn to sweep the ball off the fairway. Sweeping medium irons off Bermuda grass is the only way to hit second shots stiff to the pin or par-4 holes. (Trying to take bacon-strip divots, of the kind taken frequently on northern fairways, causes a lot of grass and dirt to intervene between the clubface and ball at impact. The result is an uncontrollable shot that flies over the green.)

Don't worry about imparting backspin on the ball. The firm Bermuda fairway mat supplies a perfect surface against which to nip the ball, creating a good amount of backspin.

To encourage a sweeping type hit, play the ball off your left heel. Balance your weight evenly be-

Sweeping the ball is the secret to hitting good medium iron shots off Bermuda grass.

tween the ball and heel of each foot. Keep your hands in line with the ball.

Concentrate on making an evenly flowing one-piece takeaway and a fluid three-quarter swing.

On the way down, think of trying to hit an imaginary ball a couple of inches ahead of the one you addressed. And you'll sweep that blade swiftly through the real ball.

SHOT
18 THE BARE-LIE BOMBER

The reason I think I strike wood shots so solidly off sparse fairway grass is that I'm an aggressive, yet controlled, hitter of a golf ball.

This is a shot made for my style because in order to hit it well you must take a divot. That's why the club player who tries to finesse this shot fails to send it flying to the green. Don't be afraid to give the ball a whack!

To get the utmost out of this shot, you must hit the ball with a sharp, descending blow. That kind of impact decreases the effective loft of the club. So if the shot calls for a three-wood, hit with a four-wood instead.

At your address, play the ball back in a square stance, but spread your feet *wider* apart than usual.

Employ a one-piece takeaway, keeping your wrists uncocked and the club's sole low to the ground until you feel the majority of your body weight transfer to your right foot. Then allow your wrists to hinge so you can swing the club back to the parallel position.

Spark the downward motion by transferring your weight to your left foot. Through impact, get the feeling that you're leading the club down with your left hand and snapping it into the rear portion of the ball with your right.

SHOT
19 THE IN-BETWEEN APPROACH

On a course with expansive, undulating greens it is very vital to be able to hit your approach shots the correct distance. If you thus fail to choose the right club, you'll land in three-putt territory, instead of lining up a short birdie putt.

I realize that club selection is not always cut and dried, a clear matter of choosing a particular iron for a particular distance. Sometimes the yardage is in-between clubs. The distance may, for example, be 155 yards, right smack in the middle of your 150 yards seven-iron and 160 yards six-iron.

The average amateur who faces this stuation tries either to manufacture a slow swing with a longer club, or hit the ball hard with the shorter club.

I advise you to select the longer club. But instead of trying to slow your natural tempo drastically, which screws up your timing, choke down on the grip and swing at your normal speed.

Set up and swing with confidence. Don't worry that choking down will cut down on your distance. Choking down actually shortens your swing arc automatically, thus your action is more compact. In effect, then, you're swinging a trifle harder.

Next time you face a similar situation and you are toying with club selection, choke down on the longer stick and hit it. Take it from Chi Chi, you won't be sorry.

20 THE SEAM SPECIALTY

Landing your ball on the left side of the fairway and facing a straight-on approach to a pin cut in the right center of the green is probably a relatively common course situation for you. However, let's pretend your ball is now resting against the seam of the rough bordering the fairway, and you face the same approach. Tricky? Well, I run into this lie from time to time, as you will, so it's best to be prepared for it.

The standard inside-to-inside swing is out because the clubhead can get snagged in the grass on the way back, causing a faulty alignment with the ball at impact. And even if somehow you bail yourself out on the backswing, rough grass is bound to intervene between the ball and the clubface at impact, causing a wild shot.

Your technical play, then, is an out-to-in swing that will impart cutspin on the ball and work it into the pin from the left side of the green. The reason for employing this method is that it allows the clubhead to avoid the rough in the takeaway. Furthermore, since you are swinging on an out-to-in path, you also avoid catching extra grass directly behind the ball at impact. Obviously, these two pluses make for a supercontrolled cut shot, provided you employ the following method of setting up and swinging.

With the ball played slightly forward of the middle of your stance, assume an open alignment. Then aim the clubface to a point in the left center of the putting surface. As a final setup checkpoint, move your hands a tad forward of the ball.

Swing up on a steep angle.

Once the club reaches the three-quarter position, pull the club down into the back of the ball with both hands, all the time maintaining your knee flex for good balance.

Through impact, your right hand should turn outward, to achieve the glancing blow needed to work the ball back to the flagstick.

21 THE DORADO BEACH KNOCKDOWN

In playing Dorado Beach, way back when, I often became frustrated when from about 80 yards out in the fairway, I hit a high shot that hit the green, then bounded over the back, either because of a very hard putting surface or a strong wind at my back. Surely you've experienced the same frustrations on the course, so let me pass on my shotmaking solution for hitting the ball stiff to the stick when playing downwind and the pin is cut close to the front of a green that's firm.

To hit the knockdown—a low shot that carries a whole lot of backspin, takes one bounce, and then settles near the hole—set up square to your target with the ball played a few inches back from your normal position for a pitching wedge. Playing the ball there places you in position to hit with your hands leading the clubhead, thereby setting up the sharp angle needed for producing backspin.

On the backswing, it's important to extend the club very low in the takeaway before continuing to swing on a shallow swing plane up to the three-quarter point.

Moving the club low to the ground and toward

52 · **101 SUPERSHOTS**

the target through impact and keeping your left hand-wrist unit firm as you sort of punch the ball are all critical downswing hooks.

SHOT
22 THE EXCAVATOR

When confronted with a ball sitting down in a divot hole, most amateurs tense up. That's their first mistake, because the body muscles have to be able to work freely during the swing. The second common error the club golfer usually makes is to play the ball forward in the stance and try to scoop the ball out. The result of that strategy is most often a topped shot.

I recommend that you play the ball nearer the right foot, so the clubface is slightly hooded at the address. That way, you're in position to hit with a very sharp *descending blow.* Remember, however, hooding the club reduces its effective loft. Therefore, if the distance normally calls for a five-iron, take a six-iron, or even a seven-iron, if the divot is very deep.

Keep the backswing steep and compact by pulling the club almost straight up in the air with your hands and arms.

Drive your knees toward the target, then pull the club through with both hands in order to hit with a forceful blow and lift the ball out and up toward the green.

When the ball is in a divot hole, don't hold back; pull the club down hard with both hands.

SHOT
23 THE DOWNHILL CHASER

By learning and applying some simple principles of cause and effect, you can approach any shot from a downhill lie with a newly found confidence and hit the ball as solidly as you do when playing off level fairway ground.

First, when confronting a "downer," you should never fight the natural tendency to lean left, because that's the very position that encourages you to align your shoulders parallel to the slope and swing along it through the hit zone; and incidentally, that's the most vital key to playing this particular shot well. (Sitting a bit back on your right leg and hip is only good when the downhill angle of the slope is very severe; off such an incline, this setup position is the only true way to regain a sense of balance.)

Second, in swinging down a slope you automatically *reduce* the effective loft of the clubface. Therefore, a good policy is to take one less club when hitting off relatively sharp downhill lies—an eight-iron instead of a seven-iron, for example.

Third, because on the downswing the upper body tends to slide with gravity, past the ball, your hands will not completely release. This slight hindrance to the releasing action causes the blade to stay open a little at impact. In turn, the ball flies lower than usual and flies from left to right. So allow for this fade pattern by aiming a few yards left of your final target.

Once you are set comfortably and correctly in relation to the ball (which should be played back slightly from its normal position to enable you to make ultimately the cleanest possible contact while

Trigger the downswing by clearing your left hip and you'll find it easy to chase the ball down a slope with the clubhead.

the club is still descending on a steep angle), swing the club back to the three-quarter position. The short action will enhance your balance, as will keeping your head almost perfectly still.

Set off the downward motion by "firing" your hips and simultaneously pulling the club down with your hands. While maintaining a steady head and deep knee flex, feel as if you are chasing the ball down the slope with the clubhead. That's absolutely the best insurance you can have for getting the ball up.

SHOT

24 THE UPHILL CLIMBER

The one governing principle for hitting a good shot off an uphill lie is to address the ball so that you can swing with the slope of the hill. Therefore, in standing to the ball, set yourself more behind it than usual. This means, you're naturally going to set more weight on your right foot than normal if you are right-handed. But that's okay; leaning hard left prevents you from setting your shoulders parallel to the slope and thus causes you to pound the ball into the hill.

During the backward motion, you must protect against swaying your body to your right, so keep your left foot planted on the ground as you employ a smooth backswing.

Because you set up with most of your weight on your right side and because you're fighting gravity when you start the downswing, it becomes difficult to shift your lower body weight to your left foot and clear your hips. Instinctively your hands roll over faster than usual, thus the clubface turns over speedily through impact, imparting right-to-left draw-spin on the ball. (To compensate for the draw, align your feet, knees, hips, and shoulders a few yards right of your target.)

For the reason that a lot of your weight is on your back foot through impact and your swinging up at the ball, the club's effective loft is *increased*. The result is a high shot. This higher trajectory dictates that you select a stronger club than you would use for a flat lie—a seven-iron instead of an eight, for example.

TAILORING THE TIP

On severe uphill lies, you'll have to make an added modification to your setup—flexing the left leg more to promote better balance.

On such a shot, you'll have to settle for less body coil and swing more with the arms. Because less turn means less power (owing to loss of clubhead speed), compensate by taking plenty of club—even two or three clubs more than normal for the distance. That way you'll swing within yourself, with excellent rhythm and tempo, and hit the ball close to the flagstick.

SHOT
25 THE BLIND PITCH

A blind pitch, to an uphill green around 75 yards away, is a very straightforward shot to hit, yet many high handicappers end up leaving the ball short of the pin or putting surface.

The two priorities on this shot, so far as strategy is concerned, are logically to get the direction and the distance right.

The easiest way to line up this shot is to walk up and see where the flag is placed on the green. Next, either line it up with a clearly visible tall tree behind the green or pick a spot at the top of the grassy bank, upon which the green sits, that is also on the path to the hole. Then when you stand over the ball and the flag is not visible, you'll know precisely where to aim your clubface.

The key to hitting this shot on the money is to allow for any dead ground between the top of the bank and where the green starts by taking more club. Remember, too, that under normal conditions a shot uphill usually requires you to hit one more club than you would normally from the same distance. From 75 yards, with 10 yards of dead ground between the top of the plateau and the green, you should seriously consider switching from a sand wedge to a nine-iron.

You'll want this shot to land softly on the green; therefore, you must: (1) Play the ball a couple of inches forward of the middle of your stance; (2) Put slightly more weight on your right foot; (3) Extend your left arm and lock your left hip, until you get a sense that your whole left side is a wall to hit against. All these keys set you up to stay behind the ball in the hitting area. As long as you then employ a smooth backswing and get the feeling of letting the clubhead pass your hands just before it reaches the ball, you'll have a relatively easy putt for a par-save or a well-earned birdie.

26 THE PITCH-AND-RUN

This shot is one the Scots supposedly invented to deal with heavy winds and hard bouncing, fast running greens. However, you don't have to be in Scotland to play it.

Here's a typical situation when a high pitch to the flag is such a risky shot that a pitch-and-run is the *percentage play*: Your ball lies dead smack in the middle of the fairway, 20 yards off the edge of a green, and 20 more yards from a pin cut on the upper level of a two-tiered green. The ball is sitting on tightly cut grass, the green is firm, and a 20 mph wind is behind you.

In lining up this shot, pick a landing spot just short of the green. Next, imagine the ball hitting it, bouncing once, and then rolling to the hole. Now you've put yourself in the mood to play this shot, which is very important for sound execution. By imagining, or visualizing, how the shot should work before you actually hit it, your mind tells your body what it has to do to make it happen.

In setting up to play the pitch-and-run, align your feet slightly closed (right foot dropped back from your left) to encourage a flat swing arc. Then aim your clubface slightly right of your final target because an exaggerated flat arc encourages you to close the blade at impact and imparts draw-spin on the ball.

Stand tall to the ball (only minimally bending at the knees and bending at the waist) to encourage an arm swing and play it back so your hands are ahead of it. The hands-ahead position decreases the club's effective loft, a key to nipping the ball and running to the hole.

Work your knees away from the target to enhance your rhythm as you swing to the halfway position with dead wrists.

On the downswing, work your knees toward the target and concentrate on keeping your hands ahead of the clubhead—a must for pinching the ball cleanly off a tight lie with a pitching wedge.

27 THE SLICE-SPIN PITCH

When the flag is cut directly behind a bunker guarding the right side of a green and hitting a holding shot is impossible due to wind conditions, I impart slice-spin on the ball. The shot I hit flies around the trap, bounces to the right, and works its way to the hole. You can increase your percentages and lower your scores by putting this shot into your repertoire. Here's how to play it:

With the ball played forward, assume an open stance and body alignment.

Swing the club smoothly back outside the target line.

Coming down, dissuade your right hand from taking over by pulling the club harder *across* the ball with your left hand.

TAILORING THE TIP

Those of you who do not play by feel will probably have trouble swinging the club back on an outside path and delaying the rollover of the right hand on the downswing. The simple solution is to hold the club with a weak grip; the Vs formed by the thumb and forefinger of each hand point up at your chin. This grip will easily enable you to employ those two previously mentioned swing tips automatically.

Still, to perfect the slice-spin pitch you must practice until you learn exactly how far you must swing back and exactly how hard you must pull the club through in order to hit the ball to a precise spot on the green.

A weak grip makes it easier for you to employ the correct, unorthodox technique required for hitting a slice-spin pitch.

28 THE HOOK-SPIN PITCH

Here's a shot that's the perfect play when you're pitching to a pin cut close behind a yawning bunker guarding the left side of the green. Moreover,

Preswing visualization and a relaxed grip are very important for hitting a hook-spin pitch stiff to the pin.

it's such a snazzy shot that playing it successfully will surely shake up your opponent.

To hit the hook-spin pitch, play the ball further back in your stance than you normally do when addressing a short pitching wedge shot. Aim right of your target and close the clubface a little before swinging back on an exaggerated inside path.

Release your right hand a little prematurely in the downswing so that it rolls over the left more quickly through impact.

Above all stay relaxed. That way the hands, wrists, and forearms work the club freely, and you don't risk hitting with an open clubface and blocking the shot out to the right.

When the shot is executed perfectly, the ball lands on the green, bounces left, and hunts the hole.

SHOT 29 THE STICK-IT-TO-THE-BALL STROKE-SAVER

Golf is a game of ups and downs, so always be prepared to confront the unexpected course situation, such as finding a twig sitting behind your ball and partially under it. In this situation moving the twig could cause the ball to move and that would mean a penalty. So hit *through* the twig.

If you're 30 to 35 yards from the green, this shot can be truly easy. All you need is the patience to set up carefully and the guts to stay down and hit the ball without peeking. If you look up, you'll hit the top half of the ball or you'll hit it fat. Either way, you'll probably score a big number on the hole.

As you set up, play the ball nearer the right in-

When a twig is touching the ball, a steep backswing will promote a sharp, forceful hit.

step, as this will encourage you to employ a steep backswing and deliver the club into the ball from a steep angle. (Because of this sharp angle of attack, the ball's flight will be virtually unaffected by the twig.) Also, stand very open, aiming your body well left of the target line. Choke down on the handle of a sand wedge for maximum swing control. And finally, lay the clubface open to program loft into the shot.

Let your right wrist hinge pretty early in the takeaway, then make a short backswing.

Rotate your knees toward the target to begin the downward motion. Ideally, you want the blade to contact as much of the ball as possible, so swing the club down pretty fast with your hands and arms.

S H O T

30 THE SEVEN-IRON ROLLER

When you face a 25-to-35-yard shot from a wet fairway to an unguarded wet green, don't risk hitting a lofted pitching wedge or sand iron. That strategy could cause you to hit the ball so fat that it lands short of the green or stops well short of the pin. Instead, guarantee yourself a good chance to save par by playing a roller with a seven-iron.

Stand pretty square to your target. Play the ball off your left heel with your hands in line with it.

Assume a strong grip by pointing the Vs formed by the thumb and forefinger of each hand up at your right shoulder. This hold will promote a flat swing plane and a sweeping hit. Therefore, you don't have to worry about hitting the ball fat—hitting a "chili-dip" shot as I call it.

To help you swing rhythmically, pull the club very gently inside the target line on the backswing. Once your hands swing to waist level, pull the club quietly through with your right hand.

The strong grip you assumed at the address

One true shortcut to hitting the seven-iron roller shot is pulling the club slowly back inside the target line.

causes your right hand to roll over your left through the impact. Don't fight it; this release movement of the right hand forces the clubhead to turn over slightly at the time of the hit, thereby imparting overspin on the ball. Consequently, you never have to worry about leaving this shot short.

The ball will land on the front of the green and roll to the hole, unaffected by the wet grass.

CHI CHI'S CLINIC

TWO ALIGNMENT CHECKS

One of the most frustrating things for a golfer is making a sound swing and hitting the ball solidly but off-line—pin high, but in trouble to the side of the green. Poor alignment is often the culprit, so here are two ways to straighten out your shot patterns.

HOME REMEDY: Stand in front of a mirror and check to see that an imaginary line running across your toes is parallel to a second imaginary line running from the ball you're addressing to a short target spot a few feet in front of you. Also be sure to check your knees, hips, and shoulders; they should be square to your target, too.

COURSE REMEDY: After assuming your address, stand straight up with the club held horizontally over the ball-to-target line. Then look down the line running through your club. You'll see immediately if you are indeed off and then be able to line up correctly to your target in seconds.

DON'T CROWD THE BALL, DON'T STRAIN TO REACH IT

Many golfers hit poor approaches because they either stand too close or too far away from the ball. The simplest solution for this problem is to stand far enough away from the ball to allow your left arm to extend in a relaxed fashion and your right arm to bend a bit at the elbow.

HEAVY STUFF

Heavy players usually have great difficulty turning their hips on the backswing and reaching the ball at the lowest point of the arc, if the ball is positioned opposite their left heel.

If you experience these problems, drop your right foot back, into a closed position, to allow your hips to coil freely and fully to about 45 degrees. Also, play the ball further back in the stance with both wood and iron clubs. It's tough to suggest an exact position, for it varies according to the player's girth. Basically, however, woods should be played about 2 inches in back of the left heel, irons about midway in the stance. Now you'll not only sweep the fairway woods and nip the irons crisply off the lush grass but you'll also get the distance you should be getting out of these clubs.

TEMPO TIP

Because a slow takeaway promotes an overall steady tempo and smooth rhythm, encourage a good start to the swing by employing some sort of forward press. Here's one that should work nicely: Gently kick your right knee toward the target a few inches, then away from it a split second before starting the club back.

Your new evenly flowing tempo will now promote cleaner hits off the fairway.

KNOW YOUR COURSE

Any uncertainty about what club to play or how hard to hit an approach shot hurts your confidence and affects your swing tempo.

One way to restore your confidence is to chart out your home-course, noting the yardage to the center of the green from a particular tree, grass hillock, trap, etc. The more spots you mark, the more likely you'll be able to pick the proper club and swing smoothly with confidence on shots from the fairway.

ALLOW FOR ADRENALINE

The typical golfer who is pumped up with confidence usually hits the ball 10 yards farther than normal.

So, if you're "up" in a match or shooting "lights out" in a stroke-play competition, protect against hitting into trouble behind the green by taking one less iron (i.e, a seven-iron instead of a six-iron) on approach shots.

WET-WEATHER ADJUSTMENTS

To discourage quickly becoming "all washed up" when playing a match in heavy rain, make this chief technical adjustment when setting up to hit an approach shot: Widen your stance to prevent slipping out of position at impact.

CURES FOR HOOKS AND SLICES

If you're hooking your approach shots from the fairway, your tempo is too quick.

Slices result from an overly slow tempo.

To *quicken* your tempo, hit a good seven-iron shot. Then try to reach the landing spot of that shot by hitting twenty-five balls with both an eight-iron and nine-iron. You probably won't reach your goal of hitting the other club as far as the seven-iron. Nevertheless, you will quicken your natural tempo because this exercise will force you to let out the shaft.

To *slow* your tempo, hit a good nine-iron shot. Then try to hit an eight-iron and a seven-iron the same distance. Now when you go out on the course, you'll gear down with all your clubs.

HOW TO STOP HITTING SHORT IRONS FAT

One common problem among high handicappers is hitting fat iron shots.

Those of you who frequently jam the clubhead into the fairway turf behind the ball should try focusing your eyes on the front of the ball rather than the back of it. This will automatically cause you to set more of your weight left at the address, which in turn encourages you to strike the ball first and the grass second.

HEAR A GOOD SHOT BEFORE YOU HIT IT

In preparing to hit a pitch-and-run off lush fairway grass, think of what a good shot would *sound* like. Try to *hear* the smooth yet crisp brushing action of the club moving through the ball and grass.

This preswing routine sends a message to your brain, and then the body responds by reproducing those sound-audible images via the correct technical movements.

PERFECTING THE PITCH

All touch players can subtly vary the length of their swings with different types of wedges, according to the nature of the ball's lie and the length of the pitch shot they face.

One simple way to build this versatility into your game is to try to hit a pitching wedge 25 yards, then 50 yards, then 75 yards. Do the same with a sand wedge and a 60-degree wedge, hitting several shots with each club out of different lies.

Through regular practice of this drill, you'll see there's nothing mysterious about learning touch.

3

OFF THE FAIRWAY

One of the things I'm most grateful for is being able to maintain my boyhood enthusiasm for golf. After all the years of playing this game, as both pastime and profession, I still get excited every time I tee up the ball. That's true whether I'm playing a casual round or competing in a championship. No doubt the man upstairs has a lot to do with my good fortune in always having fun on the course. Then, too, playing practically every week with friends on the Senior PGA Tour helps me stay happy. However, I think the game itself is mostly responsible for my neverending keenness. Whoever created this sport was a genius because once you accept that golf wasn't meant to be mastered you'll enjoy it forever.

Because I understand the ironic philosophy of golf, I accept bad shots as part of the game and actually enjoy the challenge of recovering from a trouble spot off the fairway.

Regardless of my pro status and no matter how hard I practice, there is still no guarantee that I will hit a solid, accurate drive or approach shot. But the pressure of knowing that the ball will surely land in trees or rough, should I fail to make a well-timed, technically sound swing, is what I find particularly exciting about golf. Granted, my sense of risk is not equal to that of a race-car driver who faces potential death on every turn and straightaway. Nevertheless, the constant confrontation of Chi Chi versus course provides me with nervous excitement for all eighteen holes. And I love it!

What I'm leading up to is this: In order to be a good trouble player, you first have to accept that only you are responsible for hitting an off-line shot. Getting mad only tenses the muscles and clouds the mind, thus preventing you from clearly planning a smart strategy and then putting those good, organized thoughts into action. Taking every shot in stride keeps you mentally sharp and so relaxed that your swing stays smooth and effective.

Thankfully, I grew out of the immature golfing stage a good many years ago, thus I don't ever blame the golf gods for a bad swing. I blame Chi Chi Rodriguez. I admit, when I see a shot heading for trouble I get a little peeved, but I quickly forget it. So that by the time I reach the ball, I'm ready to devote all my energy to figuring out how to get out of trouble.

I have spent hundreds and hundreds of hours practicing, therefore I know what type of setup position promotes what type of swing and, in turn, what type of swing produces what shape of shot and puts what kind of spin on the ball. Naturally, then, figuring out how best to recover from a very awkward lie comes pretty easily to me. I just tap into the bank of technical data I have stored in my brain and pick out the shot I know will work best, based on my experience and my ability to visualize what a ball will do in the air and on the ground—

before I hit it. Having these talents boosts my confidence, which is another vital ingredient to becoming a fine troubleshooter.

I've said it before, but I'll say it again: My shot-making skills are not innate. Rather, they have been nurtured from hard work on the practice ground. Take a tip from Chi Chi then, learn my trouble shots and practice them so they become a part of your repertoire for as long as you play golf.

SHOT

31 THE SIX-WOOD SMASH HIT

You golfers who try unsuccessfully to hit a long iron recovery shot out of thick, heavy rough should switch to six-wood. Whereas the thin, light head of the long iron will twist and turn, the heavy head of the utility wood will *plow* through the grass like a sickle. From as far as 170 yards out you can reach the green and give yourself a birdie putt, provided you employ a very specialized technique that I'll get into shortly. First a warning:

If the ball is sitting down so snugly that you can just barely see the top of it, don't risk leaving it in the rough grass by trying to be a hero. Simply pitch out sideways back to the fairway with a wedge.

What I guard against most, in preparing to hit the six-wood shot, is standing with my feet wide apart. This will force me to sweep the club back low to the ground in the takeaway. Normally, the sweep is a good thing to do on drives, long iron, and wood shots. However, when hitting a wood from heavy rough you need to shorten the takeaway and narrow the arc of the swing by moving the club quickly

In heavy rough you'll get maximum power out of a six-wood by actively "firing" your right side.

upward. To encourage this kind of swing, stand with your feet spread a few inches narrower than normal.

Another address adjustment that will stunt your

takeaway and narrow your swing arc is putting 60 percent of your weight on your left foot and leaving it there as you make your backswing action.

In setting up, be sure to let the clubhead hover above the ground to avoid snagging it in the grass as you go back, which is a fault that almost always ruins one's swing path, natural tempo, and shot-making goal. Also relax your grip on the club, which will promote the desired high-speed whipping action of the clubhead through the hit zone.

On the backswing, the hands should work the clubhead back, as the shoulders turn.

On the downswing, keep your head still as you fire your right hip and leg *toward the target* (as a means of helping you generate even more power), and pull the club firmly into the back of the ball.

Owing to the steepness of the backswing motion, the blow will be a sharp one, which is what will send it flying up quickly into the air toward the green.

SHOT
32 THE PERCHED-LIE RECOVERY

When the ball is sitting up high, perched on top of a tuft of grass, the average golfer is often fooled into thinking he faces one of the simplest lies possible. The fact is that it's one of the toughest shots to hit, requiring you to make certain adjustments at the address and during the swing in order to sweep the ball cleanly off the grass.

Because the ball is sitting up so high, the tendency is to hit up too much under the ball, causing you to add to the effective loft of the club. In essence then, a seven-iron becomes a nine-iron. The typical amateur golfer doesn't realize this, so he frequently hits the ball very high, landing it well short of the hole. Don't make the same mistake: If you normally hit a seven-iron 150 yards, use a five-iron from the same distance off a perched lie.

A second adjustment you must make in your setup is to strengthen your grip slightly by moving both of your hands a bit to the right. This automatically allows you to swing the clubface from an open to a closed position which ultimately guarantees a sweeping action of the club on the ball through impact. Because the ball will draw a few degrees, you should align yourself to the right of target when setting up.

The third adjustment you must make is in ball position. Play it in the middle of your stance, which is back far enough to guard against hitting up on it through impact, and far forward enough to guard against hitting with a sharp descending blow.

The fourth and final adjustment is to let your club hover above the ground just behind the ball to avoid moving it off its precarious position. On the backswing, pull the club back gently with your right hand and rotate your knees in a clockwise fashion to make the swing motion flow rhythmically. In completing the swing, keep your head steady as you turn your left hip to the left, and then fire your right side toward the target. As your hands drop down to waist height, pull the club into and through the ball.

SHOT
33 THE OFF-THE-LEAF LIFT

The trickiest part of playing this shot takes place at the address. Avoid moving a ball that sits on a leaf, otherwise be prepared to accept a one-stroke penalty for violating *The Rules of Golf*. Fearing this penalty, I never rest my club behind the ball in this situation; I let it hover slightly above the ground, just behind the ball.

Since good balance is key to playing this shot well, I flex my knees quite deeply and distribute my weight evenly between the ball and heel of each foot.

Because the ball must be *picked* off the leaf as cleanly as possible, good hand action is also critical. A light grip will greatly help you liven your hand action.

Pick the club up quickly in the backswing to set yourself up for a nice firm downswing hit. Keep the entire backswing action compact.

Drive both knees toward the target, and pull the club down and through the ball, making sure that your hands lead the way.

SHOT
34 THE FLICK

In confronting a ball lying in the rough, it's important to assess the situation very carefully, looking at the texture of the grass and its condition to see if the ball is in fact going to carry, or fly farther than normal off the clubface. If the blades of grass are dry the effects will be virtually nonexistent. If the grass is wet, you can bet the ball is going to fly at least 10 yards farther than normal and roll an extra 10 yards, too. Spotting a flyer lie is the signal to make minor changes in your setup and bigger changes in your swing, in order to give yourself absolutely the best possible chance of hitting an approach shot with an iron stiff to the flag.

Club selection is also very critical when facing a flyer. To compensate for the added yardage you'll pick up in the air and on the ground, play one less club, a nine-iron instead of an eight-iron, for example.

When setting up to play a flyer, address the ball as you normally would for a particular iron, but put more weight on your right foot. Leave it there, too, until the ball is hit, for keeping extra weight on your back foot enables you to put as much of the clubface on the ball as you can from this awkward lie, thereby canceling out the full effects of the flyer.

You'll need to generate a lot of clubhead speed in order for the club to swish through the grass and lift the ball up. Therefore, you should extend the club well back along the target line in the takeaway and turn your hips and shoulders as fully as your flexibility allows. Extending the club away will trigger a wide swing arc, which is another necessary ingredient for generating maximum clubhead speed and power. Turning fully allows you to swing the clubshaft to the parallel position, so that the hands are boosted well above your head, which further increases the width of your arc and thus enhances its power.

On the downswing, concentrate on being very "handsy." Once the club reaches the top, pull down with your right hand and sort of flick it under your left, to drive the clubface under the ball.

A good image to recall before playing this shot is one of a high exaggerated finished position. The reason for this is that striving for this end to the swing encourages you to hit through the ball with the clubface moving at high speed during the precise moment of impact

35 THE CRUSHER FROM CLOVER

Clover gives many golfers a good feeling; maybe because it's very lucky, maybe because it's very green. The irony is that landing your ball in a patch of thick clover is no lucky break. I don't care if the whole patch is full of four-leafers, skill, not luck, will play the biggest role in your ability to hit a fine recovery shot.

I think the biggest mistake amateurs make is trying to sweep the ball off the clover. This strategy leads to disaster because clover patches in the rough are usually so thick that the clubhead gets stuck for a split second going back. This false start to the swing throws off a player's rhythm and interferes with square, solid impact by shoving the blade open or closed.

When looking to reach a very long par-4 in two strokes, or advance your second shot far down the fairway on a par-5 hole, use the clover to your full advantage. Clover is very dense and its tendrils hold moisture. If you hit with a powerful descending blow you will magnify the flyer effect, because tendrils will inevitably lodge between the ball and the clubface at impact. In this case, then, when you are looking for distance the flyer lie is going to help you achieve your shot-making goal.

In setting up for the desired swing, play the ball back in your stance and put 70 percent of your weight on your left foot. Pick up the club quickly in the backswing, allowing the wrists to cock early. The motion should feel very tight knit. Keep your head perfectly still and pull the club down swiftly, while still maintaining good balance.

36 THE PLANNED HOOK

Regardless of the great amount of time I spend perfecting my swing in practice, I still make a truly bad swing occasionally, either through a fundamental technical fault or lapse in concentration. Often, the ball winds up in the rough, with a tree stupidly growing right in-between the ball and the green. No doubt, you'll eventually find yourself experiencing the same predicament. Here's the simplest way to recover.

To make the ball hook around the tree (to move sharply on a right-to-left pattern) set your feet and shoulders to the right of your target, but close the clubface by aiming the leading edge of the clubhead at the ball's final destination. Then simply swing up and down along the path set by your shoulders so that the ball starts its flight to the right. Don't worry. The closed blade imparts right-to-left spin on the ball, hooking it sharply back to the green.

TAILORING THE TIP

If you are a natural slicer I recommend that you drastically strengthen your grip by turning your

82 · 101 SUPERSHOTS

When hitting a planned hook, allow your right shoulder and side to roll left.

hands more to the right on the handle. When you look down at least three knuckles of your left hand should be clearly visible. Also lighten your grip pressure. Both of these adjustments help you to roll the right hand over your left more vigorously in the hitting area, making for a *shut blade* and hooked ball.

SHOT

37 THE PLANNED SLICE

Let's say that you have pushed your drive into trouble bordering the right side of the fairway. The lie is relatively clean, but you are about 170 yards away from the hole. Trees 20 yards up ahead block a direct pathway to the green; however, the match is such that you have to go for the green to set up a badly needed birdie.

Chances are, unless you are a highly advanced and experienced player, you have not yet learned how to hit a planned slice. Therefore, let me now teach you another new shot to put in your repertoire.

One major key to hitting a controlled slice successfully with a two-, three-, or four-iron is to let the club do the work. The flat lie, long shaft, and low loft of any higher-numbered iron club will encourage you to control the movements of the swing with your arms more than your hands. Because of this, you'll be less apt to lift the club up abruptly and pull it straight down—factors that are likely to cause the ball to fly practically straight up in the air with only the slightest left-to-right spin. That won't work—you want to put heavy slice-spin on the ball.

In setting up to hit this shot, play the ball back, as that allows you to catch the ball early in the downswing—before the clubface closes. Set your feet and body well left of the trees that obstruct your line to the green. Set the clubface at right

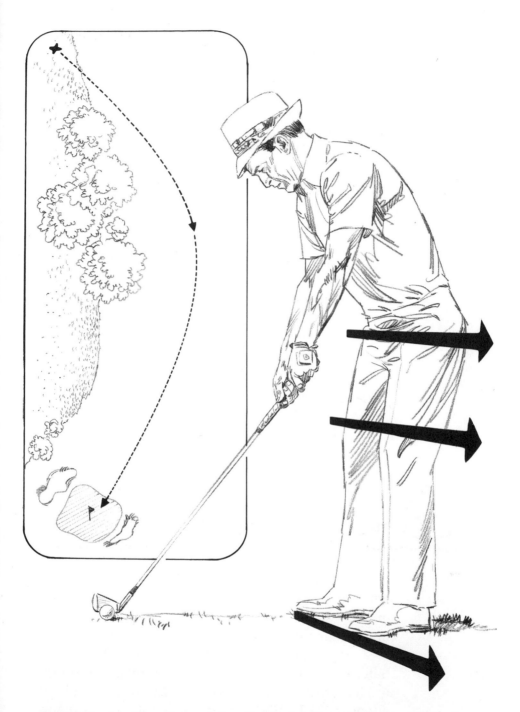

In setting up to hit a planned slice be sure to align your body well left of the target.

angles to the green, as if you were going to hit the ball straight through the trees and onto the green. The clubface is now open in relation to your body alignment. You're ready to slice.

Swing up and down on a line parallel to your body alignment. Because your clubface is open in relation to your body alignment, you cause a slicing effect at impact. The ball starts left of the trees and makes a quick right turn toward the green.

TAILORING THE TIP

If you have a natural hook, I suggest that you drastically weaken your grip by turning your hands more to the left on the handle. When you set up and look down, only one-and-a-half knuckles of your left hand should be visible. Also, grip more firmly. Those two adjustments, plus purposely swinging the club on an outside-in path, will allow you to delay the release of your hands and hit with the clubface slightly open, making for a sliced shot.

S H O T
38 THE HIGH FLYER

Knowing how to hit an extra high shot over trees will surely save you vital strokes during a round, so get the following technical tips ingrained in your muscle-memory.

Stand normally with good posture, but play the ball forward to make it easier to hit up and through it. Next, grip the club more *lightly*, since that hold allows your hands and wrists to rotate freely and promotes the upward sweeping action that you need to hit the ball high over the trees. And finally, open the face of the club and put most of your weight heavily on your right side. You'll want to keep your weight back throughout the entire swing, since this enables you to stay behind the ball, further enhancing your ability to get the ball flying quickly upward once it leaves the clubface.

Allow your wrists to hinge freely as you swing on a relatively steep angle of ascent.

Keep most of your weight on your right foot as you swing the club through briskly. This weight-back key allows you to hit with an open clubface and send the ball up high over the trees.

SHOT
39 THE TREE DODGER

To play a dartlike low shot under trees, you want to come into the ball with your hands well ahead of the clubhead and with the clubface slightly hooded to cut down its loft.

Since the type of address position you assume essentially predetermines the nature of your swinging action, play the ball off your right foot instead of opposite your left heel, where you probably normally play it. This rearward placement will force you to set your hands ahead of the ball as you assume your address, which is the perfect position for playing this particular shot. The hands-ahead position will also cause the club to rest in an ideal square but delofted position.

Drag the club away very low to the ground before swinging it upward. This type of takeaway promotes a reciprocal low follow-through, which is what's required for a low shot.

Because of the trees (and owing to human nature), you will be tempted to look up before you actually strike the ball. Do that, however, and you'll surely mishit it. Discipline yourself to keep both of your eyes *locked* on the back of the ball until you have struck it cleanly with the sweet spot of the clubface.

S H O T
40 THE SOFT TOUCH

Wiry Bermuda rough reminds me of steel wool. It's very hard to spin a ball that lodges itself in this dense grass that lines the fairways of many southern courses in the United States. Nevertheless, you can get the ball to sit down on the green pretty quickly if you switch from your normal technique to a highly unorthodox, yet easily workable swing.

To hit this shot, I address the ball with my feet, knees, hips, and shoulders aligned precisely parallel to the target line. Then rather than balancing my weight evenly on each foot I put 65 percent of it on my left foot. This manner of distributing my weight helps me propel the club on an upright arc. That arc, in turn, promotes a down-and-through hit rather than an upward sweep with the clubface at impact. Trying to sweep the ball with the clubface at impact will not work for this type of lie. You must hit down and across the ball to get it to land softly on the green.

The key to setting up a reciprocal across-the-ball downward hit is swinging the club outside the target line on the backswing.

On the downswing, keep your head behind the

ball, and pull the club down very hard with both hands. Again, because you swung the club outside the imaginary ball-target line, you'll automatically swing down and across when you're coming through.

Due to the out-to-in shape of your swing path, enough cutspin will be placed on the ball to make it land softly on the putting surface.

SHOT
41 THE OFF-THE-KNEES HIT

The average golfer sometimes takes a penalty drop when he shouldn't. Most often he does this whenever his ball lies under a bush or small tree. Granted, dropping clear of trouble and taking a one-stroke penalty is often the smartest solution. Nevertheless, don't be so quick to drop a ball until you have first carefully examined the situation and stretched your imagination, looking as hard for a shot as a lawyer does for a legal loophole.

Actually, it upsets me to see a golfer take a drop from under a tree, if I know he could have hit the ball pretty solidly and accurately by playing off his knees. Kneeling down can give you ample room to swing the club so that you'll be able to at least hit the ball down the fairway. That's better than losing a shot and then still playing from the rough.

In setting up, spread your knees wide apart, as if to build a solid and balanced foundation for swinging the club back, down, and through mostly with your arms. Let both arms stretch out, since this extension keeps your hands and wrists quiet during the action, and prevents the club from catching the ground well before contact is made with the ball. Quite a portion of the clubhead's sole will be off the ground as you jockey yourself into position. So to guarantee that you'll trap the ball at impact and make solid contact, close the face of the club a bit.

Lock your hips and swing the club back on a flat arc, being careful to let the arms control the action. Rotate your shoulders in a counterclockwise fashion while swinging your arms freely through to sweep the ball cleanly off the light rough grass.

SHOT
42 THE PIZZAZZ PLAY OFF PINE NEEDLES

Whenever your ball lands on pine needles you must exercise extreme care. Not only is the ball sitting in a precarious position, but also your footing is usually unstable.

If you intend to move any loose impediments near the ball—twigs, leaves, etc—proceed with caution. One false move could set off a chain reaction that will dislodge the ball, costing you a penalty stroke. For an identical reason, don't ever ground your clubhead when you address a ball resting on pine needles. Hold it just above the needles and be certain to grip down on the club's handle to increase your control over the shot.

To play a solid shot off pine needles, *good footing* is very important; therefore, set up firmly and carefully, in a square stance. Also, since pine needles are very slippery you must take a slightly wider stance than normal.

As a precaution against moving the ball prematurely and incurring a penalty stroke, always hover the clubhead when playing a shot off pine needles.

Make a wide flowing backswing with minimal wrist cock. This type of action will dissuade you from flicking the club through the ball and hitting a fat shot. What you want to do is pull the club down squarely into the back of the ball, with as little interference from the needles as is possible; so stay steady and wait for impact.

SHOT
43 THE HARDPAN HANDLER

Patches of worn-down ground, or hardpan, are often found off the lush fairways of golf courses. The uneducated player who hits a shot haphazardly off hardpan gets a big surprise watching his ball shoot far to the right, often into bigger trouble.

After the club has swung from inside the target line on the backswing, hardpan prevents the clubface from squaring itself to the ball. At the moment of impact the clubface is open to the target— looking right of it. Consequently, you have two choices at the address: to set up open to the target to allow for the ball's inevitable left-to-right flight (more open if the club you're hitting with features a low degree of loft), and to set up square, with the clubface toed in a few degrees, so that it faces left of the target when it's set behind the ball as a means of offsetting the blade's tendency to open at impact.

In my youth, when I experimented even more than I do today with different swings and shots, I tried to discover a way to get a solid hit on a ball lying on hardpan. When I tried to pick it cleanly off the hardpan by exaggerating the sweeping motion of the clubhead through impact, I usually topped it. This happened because the clubhead actually bounced off the hardpan into the ball.

I got my best results, and so will you, from employing a very upright backswing, which makes for a very crisp downward hit. Don't misunderstand me. You'll never feel as if you're hitting the ball as solidly as you do from fairway grass. At least with this type of swing, however, you will avoid hitting the hardpan behind the ball.

The most critical thing you must do in setting up is to set your hands 2 inches in front of the ball. Make a very short upright swing, being sure not to sway off the ball. On the downswing, encourage a full, free, fast swing, and a *whip* of the club through the hitting area, by trying to straighten your right arm.

SHOT

44 THE "STOPPER" FROM SAND

Hitting a shot out of a fairway bunker to a green about 140 yards away requires a much different technique from that used to advance a ball a good distance down the fairway. Here you want to carry the ball all the way to the green so that it lands by the hole and stops quickly. Therefore, an upright swing instead of a more rounded action is the key.

To set yourself up for the correct technique, assume a square stance, being sure to fan your left foot out a little and set the toe of your right foot perpendicular to the target line. Setting the feet down on the sand in this manner will allow you to make a powerful upright backswing and more easily clear your left side on the downswing. This hip clearance will give the arms and hands ample room to swing the club freely along the target line through impact.

You'll want to open the clubface a little so, as compensation for this preswing alteration, select one club greater than usual for the required distance. Play the ball back in your stance, so that you will ultimately catch it before the blade starts to work its way back to the inside.

Since this is virtually a total hands-and-arms shot, wiggle your feet into the sand quite deeply, but not so much as to feel you're stuck. On the backswing, set the cub early on an upright arc and stop when it reaches the three-quarter point. As you accelerate the club downward, keep your eyes riveted on a spot in the sand directly behind the back of the ball. You'll make contact early, with a slightly open clubface, because of the rearward ball position. Therefore, the ball will fade ever so slightly and set down softly on the green.

S H O T

45 THE "GOER" FROM SAND

On par-5 holes, sand bunkers set between 200 and 230 yards off the tee present a major nuisance to many golfers who land in them because the golfers have trouble advancing a second shot far enough down the fairway to set up a relatively short approach into the green. The reason is that the typical club-level player swings on too steep an angle, which is a technique that's fine for stopping the ball

Striving to get the club to arrive in the classic toe-up position is the ideal way to hit a good go-shot from a fairway bunker.

on the green from a trap, but the wrong strategy for getting the most out of a particular club.

Let's make believe that your drive on a par-5 hole has just landed in a fairway bunker featuring a relatively low lip. Your lie is good, but you have got to get the most out of the club you've selected (a four-iron), otherwise you'll face a long, tough third shot.

The ideal shot to hit is a sweeping hook, for that maximizes the distance you'll obtain because of overspin imparted on the ball and the resulting added run.

To play this shot, *wriggle* your feet into the sand only slightly. (You don't want to restrict your leg action by digging your spikes deeply into the sand.) Make sure that you set your right foot slightly in back of your left one in a "closed" position—so as to encourage a flat backswing plane. Balance your weight evenly on both feet and play the ball from where you feel you can make clean, crisp contact. Be sure to set your hands in line with the ball. (Letting them drift too far ahead will lead to a choppy action, while setting them behind the ball will cause you to hit up on it through impact. Either way, you'll come up well short of the landing spot you're aiming to hit.)

Your goals for the first half of the motion should be swinging the club on a flat plane and making a full upper body turn. To accomplish these goals: (1) Swing the club back inside an imaginary line running from ball to target; (2) Rotate your left shoulder freely under your chin.

On the downswing, swing fluidly through, so the toe-end of the club contacts the ball before the heel-end. That way, the ball will run on nicely after landing. Note: *To help you accomplish this goal, visualize the club's toe-end pointing skyward in the follow-through, before you trigger the swing.*

46 THE SURE OUT FROM HEATHER

Chances are you're a golf nut, which means that one day you'll probably play St. Andrews, in Scotland, the most historic course in the world, where the game is believed to have begun over five hundred years ago. Whether you play that famous course, or any other links, be prepared to tackle heather, a wiry purple-flowered plant that will grab the neck of a golf club and close its face as surely as a Venus's-flytrap catches flies.

A ball that lands in heather rarely perches high on the plant's upper branches; therefore, you'll usually face a tough lie that requires you to hit a pitching wedge shot back to the fairway. Don't mess with this stuff by gambling foolishly or you'll quickly chalk up strokes. Get the ball back to safety and try to make a great par or a good bogie.

In setting up for this shot, assume an open alignment and put 65 percent of your weight on your left foot. Let the clubhead hover *above* the springy-textured heather with its face open, because the gentlest touch will move the ball out of position, costing you a penalty stroke.

In swinging back, pull the club almost straight up in the air.

Lead the clubhead down into the ball with your hands.

In hitting a skipper shot across water, roll your right forearm in a counterclockwise direction and keep your head down.

SHOT
47 THE SKIPPER

Here's a miracle shot that works! The next time you hit your ball in the trees, a short-iron distance from a green fronted by a water hazard, forget trying to hit that hope-and-prayer shot through the over-hanging branches that block your line. Instead, in a tight match situation when you must win the hole, play a "skipper"—a shot that skims off the water onto the green.

Depending on the lie, select a medium or long iron. Play the ball midway between your feet and aim the club to the right of the flag as you place it behind the ball.

In swinging back, concentrate on rolling your left forearm in a clockwise direction. That will automatically get you to work the club on a flat plane.

Uncoil your right hip toward the target, and roll your right forearm in a counterclockwise direction. That movement of the arm will turn the blade of the club over more through the impact zone and thereby impart a good degree of overspin on the ball.

The ball will fly low and hard, skim across water, and roll onto the green.

SHOT
48 THE ESCAPE SHOT FROM KIKUYU GRASS

Kikuyu is an extremely thick-bladed, highly dura-ble grass that you might run into when playing a course in the western United States.

Allowing your left arm to bend on the backswing will promote the steep swing plane you need for hitting an escape shot from Kikuyu grass.

When the ball is nestled in Kikuyu, and you face a short second shot to a par-4, use a V-shaped rather than U-shaped swing to send it flying to the green.

The right hand, being closer to the clubhead than your left, is your link to power and distance control. So pick up the club abruptly with your right hand on the backswing, allowing your left elbow to bend freely.

Pull the club down with your right hand at a slightly faster speed than you use normally for a particular distance. You won't be far off the flagstick when the ball comes to rest.

49 THE LONG SANDY FROM A GOOD LIE

Your ball sits nicely in a fairway bunker 35 yards from the flagstick. The trap's lip is low and you have plenty of green to work with. What I've just described is a common yet anxiety-provoking situation for the average club golfer who falls short of a long par-4 in two shots.

Surely, this is a shot that must be practiced. However, once you get the hang of swinging on a very shallow arc, you won't back off again.

What's paramount at the address is spreading your feet wider apart and setting your hands in line with the ball, since both of those adjustments promote the proper *flatter arc* of swing.

The longer the shot, the less you should open the face of a pitching wedge and the nearer behind the ball the club should hit the sand. From 35 yards, which is normally the distance these hazards are from the green, you should set the clubface only a hair open and look intently at a contact point about a half inch behind the ball.

Extend the clubhead straight back along the target line, initially to discourage your wrists from over-hinging and thereby creating an overly narrow arc of swing. Swing no further back than the three-quarter point.

Coming through, rotate your knees toward the target and pull the club through the sand just beneath the ball. Get the sense that the blade of your wedge is skimming through the sand as easily as a knife running through butter. You should never chop down on the ball.

SHOT

50 THE LONG SANDY FROM A BAD LIE

Finding your ball buried in a bunker is disheartening, but it's worse to discover it buried in a bunker around 35 yards from the green. The latter scenario truly used to frustrate me to the point of wondering "Why me?" Then one day several years ago in Puerto Rico, while on holiday from the Tour, I made up my mind to experiment until I discovered a solution for dealing with this awful-looking lie. I tried various clubs and techniques until I indeed found a way to work magic. I found more than just a way of getting out; I found a way to hit the ball close to the hole. Provided the lip of the bunker is relatively low (if it's high, select a wedge and play out sideways), an eight-iron is the ideal recovery club.

In setting up, it makes no difference whether you set up square, open, or closed, so long as you feel comfortable. However, be sure to play the ball back to encourage the steep plane of swing you need to dig out the ball. Grip firmly with your left hand, for that hand will guide the club downward. Grip lightly with your right hand because you will be using that to flail the clubhead through the sand.

Keep the backswing short to enhance balance.

On the downswing, whip the club through by simultaneously pulling with your right hand and thrusting your knees toward the target. Contact the sand about a quarter inch behind the ball and the sharp blade of the eight-iron will take care of business. The clubhead will drive down and through the sand, popping the ball over the lip with such overspin that it will fly 15 yards and roll the remaining 20 to the green.

SHOT

51 THE FLIPPER

If you're an aggressive player you'll have to depend on a finely tuned pitching wedge game to help you salvage a good score on those occasions when your approach shot to a par-4 lands off the fairway, well short of the green.

Here's a situation you should learn to recover from: Your ball is sitting poorly in fluffy grass, on the bank of a fairway trap, some 30 yards from the green. You are forced to stand with your right foot in the sand and the other on the bank.

In readying yourself to hit, play the ball back and set your feet and body square to the target line. (Don't ever open your alignment, otherwise you'll tend to pull the ball well left of target.)

Make a slow, *controlled* backswing. On the downswing, release your hands early to flip the clubface into and then under the ball.

The ball will easily be freed from the bad lie and fly toward the pin, leaving you a short putt for par.

SHOT
52 THE PITCH FROM SANDY ROUGH

On many courses, but particularly those in Arizona, the scrubby rough is very sandy. Consequently, a 30-yard pitch off this terrible stuff presents an entirely new challenge, than the same length shot from manicured fairway grass.

When hitting out of "garbage rough," you must swing harder than you would normally to play a pitch and catch the ball more cleanly, too.

To promote solid clubface-to-ball contact, assume a narrow stance and play the ball opposite your right instep, so your hands line up well ahead of the clubface. You'll want to set yourself up for an exceptionally sharp downward blow, so leave a bigger percentage of your weight on your left foot as you employ a three-quarter backswing.

It's important that the "meat" of the clubface meets the ball before the sandy turf; therefore, keep your eyes focused on the rear portion of the ball as you pull the blade of a sand wedge down into it.

CHI CHI'S CLINIC

TRAIN THE HANDS TO WORK AS A TEAM

If you want to become a good recovery player, it's essential that both of your hands work as a team, particularly in the hitting area. Basically, the left hand should guide the club downward, while the right hand hits. Of course, the swing happens so fast that you can't possibly think about how each hand should be performing. You must, therefore, train the proper actions into your muscle-memory of your arms and hands so that during the swing they work naturally as a team.

The best training exercise I know for building teamwork in the hands is this: Swing a medium-iron twenty-five times with your left hand only, and then with your right hand only.

Practice daily and you'll not only learn to be conscious of how your left and right sides function during a golf swing, but you'll also build strength in both hands.

GUARD AGAINST SWINGING FLAT

If your backswing flattens, it will be virtually impossible for you to hit down sharply and extract the ball from heavy rough. To test that your backswing is sufficiently upright, stand about 2 feet from a wall with your back to it, then swing a medium iron up. Ideally, at the top of your swing the clubshaft should be parallel to the wall. If the clubhead hits the wall before you complete your backswing, you know your swing plane is too flat.

To correct your fault, set up with more weight on your left foot and let your elbows (right more than left) bend freely early on in the backswing.

TROUBLE-PLAY TIP

Retain this one mental hook when practicing trouble shots from dense wiry rough: Swing the hands up over the right shoulder. This one simple key will keep your action nicely upright, therefore virtually guaranteeing sharp contact of club-to-ball at impact.

THE RIGHT STUFF

To make the descending hit needed to extract the ball from various types of rough lies off the fairway, practice hitting into an old stuffed couch pillow that's firm enough to absorb the blow.

You right-handed players should set your feet outside the left side of a pillow. Next, as if addressing a ball, align the face of an iron club squarely with an impact spot on the pillow. Then swing up on a steep plane, and finally, pull down hard, with your hands leading the clubhead into the pillow.

MOLD POWER

A firm left-sided hit and hold action is essential to recovering from thick rough; therefore, to play good recovery shots, your left side must be strong. Here's a good strength-building tip for you to work on at your home or in your office:

Place the clubface of an iron against a wall molding, as if you were arriving at impact. Now, exert maximum force and hold this position for 20 seconds. Repeat the exercise five times daily.

PLAY SAFE, PLAY SMART

If you're not comfortable with the lie you confront in the rough following a wild tee-shot, aim to the safe, "fat" side of the green. This strategy is smarter than hitting the ball straight for the pin because it allows you to hit a less-than-perfect shot and still be in an easy position to save par from light fringe grass, instead of struggling to salvage par from a deep greenside bunker or from jungle rough.

4

AROUND THE GREEN

I think the short game in golf should be called the "score game." After all, the player who consistently hits the ball up near the hole, from easy and tricky lies around the green, and then holes a putt, is the one who wins more match and medal-play events.

I'm one of those golfers who depends on finesse shots to help me salvage par several times during an 18-hole round, for the reason that I, like most professionals, hit an average of only twelve greens. That statistic may surprise those of you who naïvely think pros are machines. But it's a fact.

The expert short-game player is one who must have a wide variety of shots in his bag because of the varying terrain surrounding a green. On one hole he might have a standard chip off nicely manicured grass, but on the very next hole he might be faced with a buried lie in a bunker, a delicate pitch out of rough, or a blast out of a shallow-water hazard. In golf, you just never know what challenging lie will await you once you stray off line and miss the "dance floor" with your approach shot.

The secret to developing touch, which is really

hand-eye coordination, and to not being surprised by or anxious about a strange, difficult lie is full preparation. And true preparation means trading in a fun game of golf with a threesome of friends for a heavy session of hard, honest short-game practice. Many amateurs have trouble accepting this because they have a notion that practice is boring, that it can never be challenging or amusing. Don't fall into the same futile trap. Be enthusiastic about the learning experience, be excited by the incentive that good practice will help you lower your handicap, and most of all, be willing to work. Because there is no true shortcut to becoming a short-game virtuoso, prepare yourself for putting time and effort into learning and memorizing the various techniques for hitting the many standard and sophisticated types of greenside shots I'll teach you how to play in this chapter.

Practice, however, is not all work. The fun comes from seeing how the flight and roll of the ball are affected by the club with which you choose to hit, the type of setup you assume, and also the swing you employ. How you stand, where you position the ball, the loft of the club and clubface position, and the arc and speed of your swing make a difference to the outcome of the shot.

The reward for practicing the short game diligently is being able to apply your new skills during play. If you've practiced hard hitting all kinds of shots, you'll be able to look at a lie out on the golf course and know almost immediately the best club to play, how the grass is going to affect spin, how the ball will react once it hits the green. The player who knows all those things is the one who will set up and swing correctly.

By now, you know how very important the pre-shot visualization process is. Well, it is never more important than when you are hitting shots around the green, because then you must expect to hit the ball very close to the cup, or into it. For that reason your ball-to-hole focus must be very intense, and your feel for playing any type of chip, pitch, or sand shot superb.

During a typical round, there will be some short shots that you'll have to play with dead hands and wrists. Basically, that means you swing in a pendulumlike fashion; you use your arms and shoulders to control the action and let the natural loft of the club lift the ball.

Because of much uneven, unmanicured terrain outside the green's immediate fringe area, you will often have to add loft or decrease loft to the club. That's accomplished by *leaning* your weight either well left or well right and manipulating the club with your hands, while allowing the wrists to freely cock during the backswing and uncock on the downswing.

Because of the frequency of wristy, lean shots you'll need to play, you should devote a good amount of practice to working on my two basic seesaw swings. If you do you'll find it much easier to learn the more sophisticated shots I will teach you in this chapter because they are all offshoots of these two basic swing techniques.

I lean either favorably left or right when preparing to hit almost all short shots because the way I distribute my weight dictates the flight and roll of the ball: low and running or high and soft landing. Addressing the ball with the majority of my weight on my left side, and keeping it there during the swing, allows me to hit with a hooded clubface at impact, which produces a low-running "hot" shot. Conversely, keeping more weight on my right side at address and during the swing allows me to hit down and then under the ball, which ultimately produces a high shot with a minimal amount of roll.

You might be curious about my preference for using a wristy short-game technique whenever possible and recommending that you first learn how to master it before you move on to developing a more refined repertoire of shots. So let me explain.

Begin by accepting that you have to practice a short game, no matter which method you choose to use as your shotmaking base—a wristy or wristless. But I believe wholeheartedly that you will get away with fewer hours of developing and memorizing my wristy swings because your hands are involved in producing either seesaw swing—the lean left action or the lean right action. You don't have to practice keeping your hands dead quiet, which, incidentally, is important sometimes but always a technique that feels unnatural. Besides, when you use your hands you can better work the clubhead; therefore, your feel for playing a delicate touch shot is heightened.

Generally, a wristless short-game player is less versatile, unless he has hours and hours to practice and develop finely tuned hand-eye coordination. In locking his wrists, he has to depend almost entirely on the loft of the club to hit a high or low shot. And off certain kinds of lies this doesn't always work.

My wristy method provides me with the possibility of hitting a shot higher by turning my right hand under my left through impact, thus adding to the effective loft of the club. Or I can hit even a lower, hotter shot by rolling my right hand over, shutting the clubface slightly. In a nutshell, then, using my hands lets me—and will you, too—be a better improviser around the greens.

SHOT
53 THE ROLLER COASTER

Almost every pro or amateur golfer I've ever played with has a favorite chipping club. Mine is the pitching wedge. Yours is probably the seven-iron. I think it's good to be able to feel so extremely confident with one club that you are able to play shots with it from a variety of lies. Nevertheless, you're making a very serious mistake if you reach for "your" club every time you confront a chip, no matter how different or unique the lie of the ball. For example, if your ball sits around 40 feet from the hole on bare ground, and a threadbare hillock is in between you and the hole, then you're much better off tackling this situation with the "Texas wedge"—the putter —and playing the "roller-coaster" shot.

No doubt, this advice surprises you golfers who only believe a putter is to be used on the green. Well, it can also be your weapon for shots from off the green, too, as in the course situation already cited.

Instead of taking a seven-iron or another lofted club and worrying about making precise, clean contact from a very thin lie, simply take your putter and make a dead-wristed backswing. On the downswing, incorporate a little exaggerated, lively wrist action into your stroke and make an extended follow-through. Hitting fully through will send the ball running nicely over any rough spots in the hillock and then on to the hole.

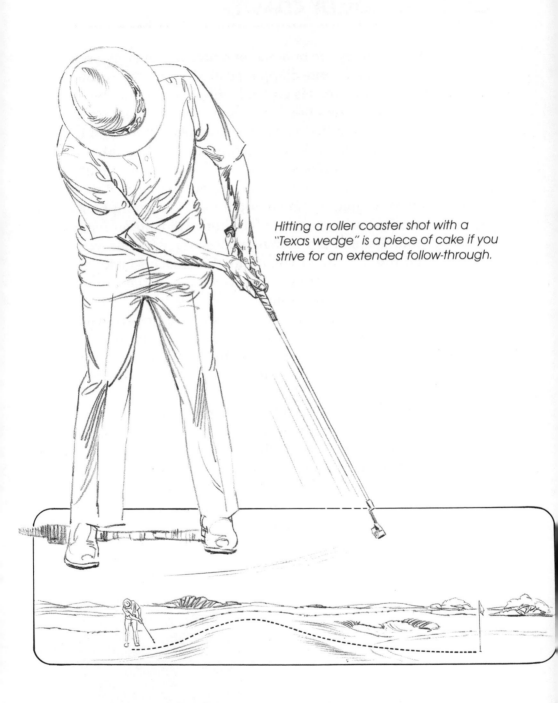

Hitting a roller coaster shot with a "Texas wedge" is a piece of cake if you strive for an extended follow-through.

54 THE SOUTHPAW CHIP

Golf is such a game of endless predicaments that eventually you will find your ball very close to a bush or tree around the green. The only thing you can do in this situation (apart from taking a one-stroke penalty and "drop") is to play a *left-handed* chip-and-run shot.

This shot is not so common that if you're a right-handed player you should start to carry a left-handed club in your golf bag. Instead, play this trouble shot with either a five- or six-iron by turning it upside down so that the toe touches the ground when you set up to hit the ball.

Personally, I taught myself this highly useful shot many years ago while looking for new shots to add to my repertoire and experimenting with various techniques. Frankly, there's nothing that difficult about learning it, provided you have pretty good hand-eye coordination and practice the following routines.

Set up in a closed position to promote an inside-square-inside swing and a gentle sweeping action through impact. Also, choke down the shaft for control and check to see that your grip is light. Holding the handle gently gives you added feel for the shot because it allows you to work the club with your hands.

In swinging the club back to about waist level, keep your right arm relatively straight. Work on this during your practice sessions because when you swing from your opposite side, there's a great tendency to bend your arm severely. If you do that, you'll pick up the club too steeply. What you want is to sweep the club away low to the ground, since that one move encourages the smooth, hit-through action you're after.

On the downswing, concentrate your energy on contacting the back of the ball squarely with the clubface. Keep the swing very short and very slow.

SHOT
55 THE RIGHT-HAND-ONLY SCRAMBLER

When the ball practically touches the base of a tree and turning the clubhead upside down to hit a left-hand shot won't give you the loft or spin you need to stop the ball quickly on a lightning fast green, try my right-hand-only shot.

Make believe the ball has come to rest by the left side of the tree's trunk. The green is directly behind you, 10 yards away.

Standing with your feet together and your back to the target, play the ball off your *right* heel. A pitching wedge is the best club for this particular shot because its short length will enhance control and its loft will give you the required soft flight and spin. To further promote control of the shot, grip down the shaft a couple of inches. Next, extend your right arm fully and lean the butt end of the shaft toward the hole.

Stare intently at the ball as you swing the wedge back to waist level, allowing your right wrist to give just enough to induce feel. (If you cock the wrist drastically, you'll inevitably hit a fat shot.)

Once you complete the short backswing motion, pull the club down rather swiftly into the back of the ball. Be sure, however, to keep your head very still and your shoulders square, otherwise you'll mishit the ball.

This lie is one you'll rarely face. However, playing my right-hand recovery shot in this tricky situation could make the difference between winning or losing a match.

56 THE BANK

Suppose your approach shot lands approximately 10 yards beyond the green—and you're confronted with an uphill pitch to a putting surface that slopes away from you. This is one of golf's most difficult situations, for there is very, very little margin for error. Rather than attempting to drop the ball delicately on the green so that it stops quickly, you should play the percentage shot—a "bump" into the bank.

In assessing this shot, I try to determine exactly how the ball is going to react by studying the texture and length of grass that covers the bank I'm hitting into. If the ground is soft and the grass thick, I hit the ball farther up the bank, because I figure it won't bounce as high and as far. The club I use to play this shot is a pitching wedge. That's the ideal club for getting the ball to bounce once before carrying to the crest of the bank.

If the ground is medium firm and the grass pretty short, I select a seven-iron. My strategy in this case is to carry the ball three-fourths of the way up the bank so it takes about two bounces before hitting the green.

If the bank's grass is sparse and the ground hard,

I play a five-iron to a spot fairly low down the bank and figure on the ball skipping most of the way to the green.

You'll want any of these bank shots to fly low. So play the ball back in your stance with your hands a couple of inches ahead of the clubhead.

The one technical point that is most critical in playing a successful bank shot is to make a short, firm-wristed swing with your arms. If you get wristy you'll tend to chop down on the ball, which will send it over the bank. So try gripping the club's handle more firmly and keep the clubhead low to the ground while going back and swinging through.

TAILORING THE TIP

If your nerves are on edge because of the pressure of the match or you lack feel in your hands on a particular day (your fingers feel fat), favor hitting the ball harder rather than leaving it on the bank. Then, if you go past the hole, you can still save a good score by making an uphill putt.

SHOT
57 THE CHOP

Since palm trees surround many of the greens on courses in the southern United States, they often offer a special challenge to the golfer who hits his approach shot off-line. If you've ever played in Florida, where I now live, you know what I mean.

Assume your ball has landed hole-high, about 20 yards from the flag. The ball is about a foot in front

Choking down on a sand wedge and leaning left will help you hit a controlled chop shot.

of the tree. In analyzing the lie, you know right away that the tree will prevent you from standing normally and making a normal minipitch swing. Worse still, if you rebound the ball off the tree the tree's texture is too rough and uneven to guarantee a clean ricochet. How do you recover? Play my chop shot using a sand wedge.

Because you are so near the tree, you'll need to create a super-steep swing in order to pop the ball up high into the air and then onto the green. The easiest way to promote such a narrow swing arc is to choke down on the club's handle, so that your right hand grasps the steel shaft. This will encourage you to stoop over more from the waist, which in this case is good for it promotes a steep backswing, as does leaning most of your weight left.

Once you are set up to play the ball, let the swing just happen. Your unorthodox grip and posture will cause your wrists to cock and uncock very dramatically and the club to move on a steep angle of ascent and descent. So just keep your head steady until you *hear* the impact. Then look up as the ball flies softly toward the flag.

SHOT
58 THE ROADWAY RECOVERY

On some of the older courses around America dirt cart paths have not been paved with tar, so the golfer whose approach lands on one of these is often not (according to a "local rule") entitled to a free lift and drop. He must play the ball as it lies.

Pretend you're in a similar spot (and if you don't run into this type of lie at your home course, you can bet you will sooner or later at a friend's course or when you travel abroad to Scotland, England, or Ireland). Your ball sits on a trodden-down dirt path to the side of a green—pin high. There are 5 yards of heavy rough between your ball and the green. The distance from the green's edge to the cup is 10 yards.

The rough is an obvious hindrance, so putting the ball is out. For that same reason, chipping is not a logical choice either. In fact, even a pitch with a sand wedge won't work because the bounce on this club will cause the blade to skid into the ball. You'll therefore skull the ball—fly it low and hard—across the green. What's left is a cute little roadway recovery played with a pitching wedge.

With the ball played midway between your feet in an open stance, bend over more than normal from the waist to encourage a very short, very upright swinging action. Increase your knee flex because it's especially important to stay fully down while hitting this shot. Also, weaken your grip to encourage a shut-to-open movement of the clubface.

Pick the club up quickly with your hands, while exaggerating the hinging action of your right wrist.

Pull the club down into a spot just behind the ball, so the wedge's sharp leading edge nips the ball off the dirt path. Minimize the follow-through.

SHOT
59 THE PARACHUTER

Nowadays, some new courses feature grass bunkers around the green instead of sand bunkers. Not only does this new hazard make golf even a bigger and better challenge, it also saves on high maintenance costs. Chances are, then, that it won't be long before grass bunkers become part of the regular golfing scene. Let me give you a preparatory lesson on how to recover from one of these.

The lie of the ball will determine the nature of your stance and swing. Since grass bunkers usually sit greenside and are allowed to grow in (unlike the finely manicured fringe of the green), the ball will usually be sitting down pretty snugly. In recovering from such a lie, a more exaggerated *open* stance is needed to promote an upright out-to-in swing path, which in turn sends the ball flying softly to the pin.

To further program height into your swing, open the blade of a sand wedge just slightly and play the ball a hair forward of your left heel. Swing the club up on a steep angle, but try to keep your motion short as an aid to controlling the shot. On the downswing, drop the clubhead down easily so that its leading edge contacts a spot just behind the ball. This accelerating action will allow you to pop the ball into the air so that it will fall softly to the green as if it were connected to a miniature parachute.

60 THE LOB

●●

I think that hitting short touch shots is even more important to scoring today than it ever was before. The reason is that many modern courses feature fast, undulated greens. When the greenskeeper puts the flagstick on a small plateau among the greens slopes, it often makes the landing area for a shot look about the size of a dish towel.

When you're a few yards off the green and pitching to a pin cut on a plateau, hit a soft lob shot with a sand wedge. If the lie is tight, consider a pitching wedge.

To execute this shot, set the clubface back more than normal at address to *increase* its natural loft. Next, grip more firmly with your left hand and maintain that secure hold in the hitting area to discourage your right hand from turning over and closing the clubface at impact.

Swing the club straight back from the ball and then up once the weight of the club forces your wrists to hinge.

Finally, uncock your wrists and throw the clubhead gently toward the ball before sliding its open blade under it.

TAILORING THE TIP

Here's a lesson for those of you who have difficulty playing this shot by feel: Encourage the sliding action of the club under the ball by keeping your head back, behind the ball, until after impact.

SHOT
61 THE SUPER-CUT LOB

This is a greenside shot I and most of my fellow pros depend on most when there is a hazard between the ball and the pin. Since you'll probably find yourself in this same position during a round, it pays to learn how to hit the super-cut lob shot and practice it until you perfect it.

The ideal club for the shot is a sand wedge. You'll want to open the clubface about halfway from a good lie, and more if you figure quite a bit of grass will get in between the ball and blade at impact.

In addressing the ball, which should be played well forward, stand exaggeratedly open with your feet's line set well left of the target line. Place a trifle more weight on your right side and leave it there throughout the swing, since this will help you hit the ball softly into the air.

Swing the club up *outside* the target line, then pull it across the ball, keeping your left-hand grip firm. To ensure that you produce a floating shot that stops quickly on the green, allow the club's heel-end to lead its toe-end into the finish.

Practice this shot until you learn to accelerate the clubface underneath the ball. Trust that the club's loft will pop it into the air. Trying to help the ball up, or getting tentative through impact, will only lead to a skulled shot that never rises above the grass, let alone the hazard you're trying to overcome.

To hit a super-cut lob that stops quickly next to the pin, swing the club on an out-to-in path.

A scooter shot is often the answer when a shallow sand trap is between the ball and the hole.

SHOT
62 THE SCOOTER

Suppose your ball is resting to the side of a green and a shallow sand trap blocks your clear path to the hole. The lie is bare and you have a minimal amount of green to work with. In looking over the situation you determine that a standard pitch shot will skip past the hole. *What do you do?*

The solution for saving par is to run the ball through the trap so it reaches the green with just enough speed to roll within a one-putt range.

This is such an exacting shot that correct club selection is an obvious priority. The distance between the ball and the trap, the width of the trap, the texture of the sand, and whether or not there's a grassy fringe to be crossed on the other side of the trap are all variables that have to be considered when you try to choose the right club.

Most of the time the sand is soft. That's my signal to have my chip shot carry across most of the bunker before hitting the sand and scooting onto the green. The best club for achieving this shot-making goal is either a six- or seven-iron. Experiment with both in practice to see which club works best for you.

Use exactly the same technique as you do when you play a basic chip; however, in this case, play the ball farther back than usual to encourage your hands to lead the downstroke. You'll then hit the ball with a hooded clubface and be ensured against popping it up so that it'll fall short and be left in the sand.

63 THE DIGGER

If you're hitting about a 20-yard shot down to a green from a fairly steep downhill lie, it's doubtful that you can hit the ball high enough to stop it on the green—unless you play the "digger."

The digger is a funny shot in that it's actually a *fat* shot hit on purpose with a pitching wedge. However, when the turf is relatively soft and the situation is as I previously cited, employing the digger is the only way to get the ball to fly slowly off the clubface so that it sits down right away once it lands on the green.

To set up to play this shot, play the ball forward in a very open stance, with your hands behind it. Open the clubface so wide that it practically lies flat on the ground.

Make a short, steep backswing.

The key to the downswing is *cutting* a slice of turf behind the ball. The easy, most efficient way to do that is to swing down hard—to China!—while keeping your knees very flexed.

64 THE SPLASHER

The next time your ball lands in a water hazard close by the green, don't be quick to pick it out and take the one-shot penalty. If a good portion of the ball is visible (at least half of it) and your footing is relatively firm, your chances of hitting a fine recovery shot are excellent.

Because hitting the ball up in the air with kind of a dead flight is paramount, select a good wedge to do the job. Unlike the pitching wedge, which will probably dig too deeply into the mud because of its sharp leading edge, the sand wedge's bounce will prevent that from happening.

When setting up for this shot, stand open and play the ball relatively forward in your stance. Playing the ball up allows you to stay behind it more easily through the hitting area, which is key to lofting it softly to the green.

Open the face of your club a hair (more, if you're less than 10 yards away) to further promote height. Swing the club halfway to parallel, using a loose action. (You might want to purposely tilt on the backswing to leave most of your weight on your left foot, instead of transferring it to your right side as you often do.) Tilting, or rocking left, as you swing back encourages you to move your weight to your right on the downswing. That of course is the opposite of your normal weight-shifting action; however, it will work wonders on this shot.

Once you are wound up, just swing the club down with your hands and arms, while keeping your eyes locked on the ball. So long as you tilted on the backswing, the rest of the swing will run on automatic pilot.

SHOT
65 THE RUNNER

•••

When the ball lies in fringe grass fronting the entrance to a green, and the pin is cut on the top tier, high handicappers often mistakenly select a pitching wedge to play the shot. Every time I witness this error in club selection, I feel compelled to scream, "stop!"

The typical player who tries to carry the ball onto the green's upper level with a wedge usually makes one of two mistakes: He pitches the ball too short and fails to reach the green's top tier, or he carries the ball too far and thus faces a second chip back to the hole.

Although the pitching wedge is a very useful club in many greenside situations, it is not what you should be playing here. The percentage play (which will leave you a relatively easy par putt) is to run the ball up with a six-iron.

The idea is to get the ball rolling as soon as possible on the green. To accomplish this objective, keep your hands *ahead of the ball* at address. Also grip more firmly so as to deactivate your wrists. You don't ever want them to get overly loose, otherwise you'll tend to come down on the ball from too steep an angle and consequently mishit the shot.

As you sweep the club virtually straight back along the target line and low to the ground, keep your leg action quiet and lock your hips.

The proper feeling on the downswing should be one of *raking* the ball to the hole as you swing the club through in a pendulum fashion with locked wrists.

If the hands lead the clubhead in the hit zone, the ball will pitch on the green, bounce, then run to the hole as smoothly as a solidly struck putt.

66 THE JAB

On many short courses, the greenskeeper lets the grass grow quite long around the greens to make it more of a challenge. So if your ball lands in this "junk" and is surrounded by grass, you'll have to do some heavy concentrating and Houdini-like improvising.

In such a greenside situation, you must first determine what club will loft the ball out, land it on the edge of the green, and roll it softly to the hole. The answer to this on-course problem is usually the sand wedge. The shot is a jab.

To play it, I recommend that you assume either an open or square stance. Never align yourself closed in this particular situation. That setup would ultimately cause you to impart an exaggerated degree of overspin on the ball, causing it to run well past the hole. Here, from 20 to 25 feet away from the pin for example, having so little green to work with, you want backspin not overspin.

To achieve the desired result—a soft flying ball that lands gently and rolls slowly to the cup—swing the club almost straight up in the air and outside a direct line to the target.

With minimal body movement, pull the club down and across the ball, keeping the follow-through short. Get the feeling that you are popping the ball out by using a stabbing action—a short, quick *jab* with the clubhead. Don't worry; the grass cushions the blow and the ball pops out softly.

Practice until you can vary the distance by controlling the swing speed as I do. Then you'll be fully prepared to hit this type of match winner under pressure.

67 THE UPSLOPE MINIPITCH

Probably one of the easiest shots to play is a miniature pitch off an uphill grassy bank; yet many amateur golfers have problems playing it because they

*The wrists must stay locked in
the hitting area when you're
playing a minipitch off an
upslope.*

try to scoop the ball out of a snug lie by using an overly loose, sloppy swinging action. Don't do that.

In setting up for this recovery, play the ball forward in an open stance. Lean into the slope and be sure to turn in the face of your sand wedge to allow for its opening when it contacts the grass at impact.

Going back, keep your weight left and make a short, *wristless* swing.

Coming down, keep your wrists locked and concentrate on swinging up the slope. This upward action allows you to increase the effective loft of the club, thus you're better able to free the ball easily and loft it softly to a landing spot close to the cup.

S H O T
68 THE POP

When your ball sits pretty deeply in spongy greenside grass, a relatively short distance from the hole, hit the pop shot with a sand iron.

You'll need to employ a very upright handsy backswing, so play the ball back and bend more than normal from the waist. Choke down on the club and grip it lightly. This is a flyer lie of sorts, so slow down the speed of the ball by trying to land it in the light fringe.

Another key to slowing down the ball is slowing down clubhead acceleration. So when you swing down don't pull on the club hard with your strongest hand—your right. Let your weaker left hand guide the blade under the ball. That's the best way to keep the clubface open to its maximum at impact, which is what you'll need for going under the ball and hitting high.

In hitting the pop shot out of deep, spongy greenside grass, it's very important that you freely cock, or hinge, your wrists on the backswing.

It's okay if the club fails to cut through the grass. Just giving the grass behind the ball a gentle hit with the clubhead will be enough to *pop* the ball to the fringe only a few feet away.

SHOT
69 THE BULL'S-EYE CHIP

● ●

Your ball is pin high in the fringe 35 feet from the hole. The green is level but lightning fast. You need to hole out for birdie to win the match.

You can play this shot with a variety of clubs; I think your best bet, however, is an eight-iron. This club features sufficient loft to get the ball onto the green and running like a perfectly rolled putt once it lands. A pitching wedge, sand wedge, or nine-iron are all risky choices, because the added loft built into the clubface of each of these clubs could cause you to leave the ball well short of the hole. Remember, you've got to hit the ball *into* the hole.

The two most important aspects of your setup must be assuming a narrow open stance and being sure that your left arm forms a straight line with the clubshaft. An open stance will give you a clearer picture of the target than you would get from assuming either a square or closed stance. Keeping your left arm and the clubshaft in a line will give you a sense of oneness with the chip stroke.

The key to the backswing is to preserve the triangle formed by an imaginary line that runs down both of your arms and across your shoulders, while keeping your wrists quiet and swinging the club back to about waist height.

To achieve the optimum directional control needed to hit the bull's-eye, pull the club gently down with your left hand. Get the feeling that the back of your left hand is moving toward the target and your right hand is behind it. Working the knees toward the target will help you maintain good rhythm and tempo so that you get the distance just right. The ball will carry the fringe, land softly, and roll to the hole—and then into it!

SHOT

70 THE REBOUNDER

When the ball is resting so near a tree trunk that you can't make a left-hand or right-hand-only swing, and you can't face the target, don't think the only recovery is a chip hit sideways or a penalty drop. You just may be able to rebound the ball off the trunk and onto the green. Here's how to save par the hard way.

Select a seven-iron. This club promotes confidence, makes it easy for you to play off bad lies, and allows you to hit the ball high enough on the tree trunk to give you the required soft flight and roll.

Face the tree with your entire body set left of its trunk, or you'll risk getting hit with the ball once it ricochets off a smooth area of bark. Make a very slow, very controlled swing, keeping your wrists quiet. Not using your wrists actively enhances your control of the clubhead, thereby allowing you to hit the ball into a spot you picked out on the tree's trunk.

SHOT
71 THE DOWN-AND-DIRTY HIT

This shot, when mastered through hard, honest practice, will cut vital strokes off your score because it's very effective when your ball lies in a patch of soft dirt in the rough to the side of a green, about 15 yards from the flagstick.

It's too risky to try to play this particular shot like a chip. Even I wouldn't try that strategy; I'd be afraid of hitting the ball too fat and dropping it in tall, troublesome fringe grass close by the green.

You want to send this ball softly into the air, which means you must play a high-lofted sand wedge and set up the following way to promote a very upright backswing and sharp, descending hit.

Open your stance and distribute a high percentage of your body weight on the ball of your left foot. Play the ball in the middle of your stance. Set your hands two inches in front of the ball. Without shifting any weight to your right side, swing the club up quickly, with pretty much a maximum wrist cock.

On the downswing, rehinge the wrists and pull the club down with your left hand; you should be grasping it firmly with your last *three fingers*.

To guarantee relatively clean clubface-to-ball contact and also ample height and bite, it's vital that the downswing arc stays unbroken as the clubhead is pulled through the ball.

72 THE FRINGE-BENEFIT CHIP

Golf is truly a game of inches, so don't ever be surprised if you hit a ball just over a green and find it resting against the seam separating manicured fringe and rough. In such a position, it's difficult to drag the putter back low and make a smooth overall stroke. The tendency on the part of the average player is to lift the putterhead abruptly upward and stab the ball coming through.

Should you find yourself in this predicament, a better choice of club is a sand iron, because its heavy flange is especially designed to glide through the grass.

To hit this shot, take a narrow stance, very similar to the one you probably use for putting. Next, choke down and make the blade hover slightly above the grass so that the club's leading edge lines up with the *center* of the ball.

Employ a stiff-wristed arms-and-shoulders pendulum backstroke. *Accelerate* the clubhead through so that the wedge's leading edge contacts the ball a tad above its equator. To your surprise, you'll find that the ball actually rolls as purely as a putt.

73 THE SLIDER

This is the call when your ball lies in dense, wiry greenside rough, and you have very little green to work with.

The ultimate goal here is to hit behind and under the ball with the clubface wide open at impact. Avoid hitting down on the ball with a hard blow, otherwise it will shoot off the clubface and fly over the green. Remember, flyers result from grass

In readying yourself to play a slider shot, be sure to set your hands behind the ball.

getting between the grooves of the club and the dimples of the ball at impact. Again, *sliding* the blade under the ball is the key to hitting a winner in this ticklish situation.

In setting up for the slider shot, play the ball midway between your feet with your hands *behind* it. Your stance should be narrow to encourage an upright swing. You should set more weight on your right foot and leave it there throughout the action. This adjustment best enables you to throw the blade under the ball at impact.

You should relax your right-hand grip, since that enables you to hinge your right wrist quickly and more easily on the backswing, which is paramount for precise execution.

Once you're set, simply swing up on a steep plane. Then swing down, rolling your right hand *under* your left as you accelerate the clubface under the ball.

To hit the ball extra softly, so that it stops quickly near the hole, make your right palm practically face the sky at impact.

SHOT
74 THE SAND CHEATER

Sometimes, even on the most finely manicured courses, your ball will be found lying on a firm, sandy spot in the fringe. In facing this situation, don't fall into the trap of choosing a seven-iron and trying to pick the ball cleanly off the ground, as so many average club players do. If you make that mistake, nine times out of ten you'll mishit the ball. This isn't as tough a shot as it appears, so long as you select a third-wedge and let this club's 60 de-grees of loft do most of the work for you.

At address, set up open to your target, with the ball very far back in your stance and your hands well ahead of it.

Two big preswing keys for recovering from a sandy spot in the fringe are to select a 60-degree wedge and play the ball back.

The secret I've found to playing this shot well is to stay *firm* with the wrists as you swing the club back a tiny bit outside the target line and up to only about knee height. I've found that if you get too wristy on this shot the backswing steepens, which causes you to hit too hard.

Keep the wrists dead as you pull the clubface down into the ball. Although both of your hands pull down, you'll find through practice that the best results come from a firm left hand guiding the club down, followed by a firm right hand doing the hitting.

75 THE TRAP

When my next shot is a 60-foot chip from relatively heavy fringe grass, and the green I'm hitting to is very slow, I plan on trapping the ball with a sand wedge, as you should, because that is the simplest way to control the shot in this particular situation.

Actually, you need super control, super feel, and super balance to play this shot. So choke down on the club and hold the handle lightly in your fingers.

Take a square stance and spread your weight evenly between your feet to enhance balance. To encourage a descending hit, play the ball back in your stance and keep your hands slightly ahead of it. To ensure that you trap the ball, hood the face a bit.

Swing the club back on an *outside* path, allowing your wrists to hinge naturally.

Upon completion of what your own personal feel tells you is the proper length backswing, uncock your wrists so that the clubhead is snapped back down and the clubface traps the ball. Minimize the follow-through.

If you kept your head still and timed the trapping action just right, the ball will rise out of the heavy fringe, fly low, land, and then roll to the hole.

SHOT
76 THE PITCH-PUTT

Your ball is sitting fairly cleanly in fringe grass bordering the green. Nevertheless, you are only 3 feet from the green's edge closest to you and 8 feet from the hole. Therefore, a chip with a seven-iron is out of the question. That club does not have enough loft to help you hit the ball high enough for it to land softly on the green.

Instead, you need to flip the ball onto the green with a pitching wedge. One key to hitting this nifty little shot is to let the club's loft do the work for you. There is no need to manipulate the clubhead in a fancy fashion with your hands.

To allow the pitching wedge's 52 degrees of loft to take care of business best, hold the club with a *reverse-overlap* grip by draping your left forefinger over the pinky of your right hand. This grip encourages a firm up-and-down swinging action.

Swing the club straight back and through along the target line, using your arms and shoulders to control the motion. Since power is not a priority here, there's no need for a big turn of the upper body going back and a lateral leg thrust coming through. A pitching wedge and a short, accelerating putting stroke is all you need.

77 THE FLAGSTICK FINDER

Let's say that your second shot on a par-4 hole fin-ishes behind a small greenside hillock. Over the hillock is a green that slopes away from you, and the cup is cut only 10 feet in from the edge closest to you. The thought of this situation probably scares you, but it won't any longer if you practice the fol-lowing recovery technique, using a sand wedge.

Soft hands are necessary on this shot, because on the downswing you want to drop the clubhead down gently into the grass behind the ball. So grip lightly with both hands, but even more so with your right, which is your ultrasensitive hand closest to the clubhead.

Spread your feet apart narrowly to promote an upright swing arc. Program loft into your shot by playing the ball forward. Swing the club up using minimal hand and wrist action. Stop when your hands reach chest height.

Swing the club down with your arms. To help the blade glide smoothly under the ball, with the full loft of the sand wedge being maintained, retain your good *knee flex.*

The ball will float over the grassy bank and roll gently down the slope to the hole.

78 THE CLOSED-CLUBFACE CHIP

Controlling the run of the ball is an important key to becoming an expert short-game player. In fact,

When hitting a ball over a hillock and down a slope to the hole, enhance your balance by maintaining that good knee flex.

being able to put some stuff on the ball, or take it off, is the critical link to *feeling* a shot.

Hitting off the heel of the clubhead closes its face, thereby causing the ball to fly low and run toward the hole after landing. So you should employ this technique if you have about 15 yards of finely cut fairway between you and an extremely firm green, and when the pin is cut close in toward its front edge. Because a high wedge shot will probably bound over the green or finish well by the hole, play a running chip with a nine-iron, using my closed-clubface method.

Play the ball back in your stance and off the heel of your club. Put the majority of your weight on your left foot. As you extend the club back on an inside path (don't pull it up too quickly) with almost no wrist cock, keep your upper and lower body pretty still.

On the downswing, get the feeling that you're swinging out at the ball, encouraging heel-first contact. The ball will fly low, hit the fairway, bounce a couple of times, then roll onto the green toward the hole.

SHOT
79 THE OPEN-CLUBFACE CHIP

You might want to try this shot when you're on the fringe chipping to a very speedy green that slopes severely away from you. Hitting off the toe opens the club at impact, so the ball flies high, lands softly, and rolls with "die-spin."

Select a sand wedge, and take your normal chipping setup. Play the ball midway between your feet, and position it off the toe of the clubface. Swing the club back on an upright angle, allowing your wrists to cock freely.

On the downswing, keep most of your weight

on your right side, and concentrate on swinging to the left of the flag. Doing that ensures that the clubface's toe-end contacts the ball first. That impact will open the clubface and cause gentle cut-spin to be imparted on the ball.

80 THE BANGER

Here's the situation: Your ball sits so snugly in Bermuda-type grass bordering a green that only the top half of it is visible. You must carry the ball only 3 feet to reach the green and roll it another 20 feet to the hole.

I'm going to surprise you now by telling you that the ideal club for this lie is a putter. Unless you really do well playing by feel and can expertly manipulate the blade of a wedge in such a way as to impart an extra-exaggerated spin on the ball, then the play is a banger with the putter. Hit this shot and the ball will pop over the fringe, take one short bounce, then roll all the way to the hole like a putted ball. Let's look at the ins and outs of playing it well.

With the ball played midway between your feet, stand relatively square to your target. Playing the ball back promotes a very upright backswing and sharp downswing hit from a steep angle, as does stooping over from the waist and leaning more of your body weight left.

In assuming your grip, make it "weak" by turning each of your hands more toward the target. (This hold will discourage you from swinging on too flat a plane, thereby preventing a mishit.)

In playing a banger shot with a putter, trigger the backswing by cocking your right wrist.

To guard against snagging the putterblade in the grass going back, let it hover behind the ball. Cock your right wrist immediately and make a stunted backswing.

To trigger the downward motion, quickly *uncock* your right wrist. That action causes the putterblade to bang down hard on the top half of the ball. Because the key to this downswing is to stun the ball with a hit-and-hold technique, don't try to follow through.

SHOT
81 THE HALF-AND-HALF HOLE SEEKER

•••

The ball is sitting partially in sand, partially in grass just behind a big bunker that sits between you and the green. It lies 70 feet from the hole. The pin is cut 20 feet from the fringe.

I've just described what is perhaps one of the top ten toughest lies for both professional and amateur golfers. This situation scared me to death in my early days. Not now; I know how to play it. Here is how.

Plant your left foot solidly by digging it in the sand. The toes of your right foot, which rests on the grass, should be perpendicular to the target line to prevent you from swaying off-balance on the backswing.

Make sure the ball is forward and your head is behind it, too, since those positions will help you gain height with a pitching wedge. To further promote height, open the blade of the wedge halfway as you settle into your address.

Swing up to the three-quarter position making a loose, free action. Pull the club down with both hands and *splash* the sand with its leading edge, a half inch behind the ball. Be sure to follow through fully, so that your belly button faces the target.

Don't try to get cute with this shot. To reach the hole, you must swing aggressively. You can afford to do that because you hit behind the ball with an open clubface.

SHOT
82 THE CHIP FROM SAND

The sand wedge is one of the most versatile clubs in the bag; therefore, I use it a lot of the time for hitting finesse shots around the green. The truth is, however, that it isn't what some golfers think is *the* club to use when their ball lands in sand.

Often, when the trap's lip is low and there are 20 to 30 feet of green to work with, a chip with a short-iron is a much better strategy. The bonus: You don't have to worry about taking such a precise amount of sand as you must when you blast a ball from a bunker.

I normally play the ball back slightly in my stance (more if the lie is not perfectly clean) so that my hands automatically line up ahead of the clubhead at address—which, incidentally, is a position I want to repeat at impact.

Assuming an open alignment gives my arms freedom to swing the club back and through more easily and freely. Putting about 60 percent of my weight on my left foot helps me *nip* the ball off the sand.

The idea is to make a one-piece hands-arms-and-shoulders stroke at a steady tempo. Strike the ball just a fraction harder than you would if you were chipping from grass.

83 THE DOWNHILL PUTT FROM SAND

When you have a clean lie in a greenside trap, but your ball is sitting dangerously on a very severe downhill slope, you should play a putt shot, provided the lip is low. Since explosions off treacherous downhill lies are nearly impossible to control, the putt is the smart play.

If the sand is relatively soft, the bunker putt is hit essentially the same way as a regular putt, requiring only two minor adjustments, one in *setup,* the other in *stroke.*

When assuming your address, grip down on the shaft an inch or two, to guard against resting the putterhead on the sand and thereby incurring a two-stroke penalty.

You'll find that digging your feet in the sand will encourage you to swing the putterblade back and through with your arms and shoulders. That's good. A wristless stroke minimizes your chances of hitting behind the ball. As to the adjustment in your stroke, simply hit the ball twice as hard as a putt of the same distance on a green. This compensates for the ball's somewhat sluggish roll through the soft sand.

TAILORING THE TIP

A putted ball will roll very quickly over hard sand, especially down a slope. To make an allowance for this speedy surface, swing the putter on an out-to-in path. Such a stroke will impart cutspin on the ball, thus slowing its speed to the hole.

84 THE SOFT EXPLOSION

Being a successful bunker player isn't about learning and memorizing one basic method. You will confront varying lies in sand, all of which require a slightly different technical solution. Nevertheless, let me first show you how to hit the normal explosion, since that's undoubtedly the shot you're most often going to be called upon to play.

The majority of sand bunkers that sit greenside don't cover all that wide an expanse of space, so you'll usually be hitting this shot to a flagstick about 25 to 30 feet away. Normally, too, the lie will be good and the lip relatively low.

The essence of the explosion technique is to make a very shallow entry into the sand with the clubhead. For this reason, it's important that you set up to make a shallow U-shaped swing arc by assuming a wide stance and distributing your weight equally between the toe-end and heel-end of each foot. Also, playing the ball forward is critical for shaving a fine cut of sand, so work around a position opposite your left instep.

Once you've settled into your setup and have the clubhead hovering over a contact spot about an inch to an inch-and-a-half behind the ball make a smooth backswing.

Swing down, gently slapping the sand with the clubhead's sole. Strive for a high follow-through. The club should swing on a path that's similar to that of a normal pitch shot, rather than the unorthodox out-to-in path usually associated with more sophisticated sand shots. The result is a shot where the ball is clipped relatively cleanly from the sand, just as if you were hitting off a plush wool carpet.

This technique is most effective in a trap with a *light layer* of sand over a base of firm soil. It also allows you to stroke nearer the ball, which enhances your feel for the distance. Spending some time practicing this shot will be very worthwhile, even if it means canceling a golf date or two until you gain a good feel for playing it.

You must swing the club along a shallow arc to hit a great explosion shot from sand.

85 THE BALL-IN, FEET-OUT SAND BLAST

Even I find it awkward to stand outside of a bunker to blast out a ball. That's precisely why I practice it every chance I get, and so should you.

Good balance is the most vital key to successfully executing this shot. So really get down to the ball, flex your knees until you feel secure, then bend at the waist to lower your shoulders.

In order to maintain a posture that feels secure and also to take the correct cut of sand under the ball, you must make a rhythmic, compact swing, controlling the action predominantly with your arms. Cut back the coiling action of your upper body on the backswing, or you'll tend to uncoil too aggressively, stand up on the shot, and blade the ball over the green.

Focusing intently on a contact spot behind the ball (which will vary according to the distance) will dissuade you from swaying, thus you'll make a controlled backswing. Furthermore, it will help you stay down through the hitting area and take a nice even cut of sand.

86 THE GLANCING BLOW

Sometimes during a round of golf I'll look at numerous tough, tricky pin placements and think to myself: The head greenskeeper must have had a fight with his wife last night.

One of the toughest spots for me to be in on the course, and one you'll no doubt run into one day, is this: The ball is sitting down slightly in a very high-lipped greenside bunker. You are about 20 feet from the pin, which is cut on a crown (small plateau) of a big, severely undulating green.

Frankly, this is an all-or-nothing situation. Either get the ball to land on the crown and stop, or miss it and face a long, treacherous, sloping putt.

To get the ball up high over the lip and then onto the plateau where the cup is cut, you must impart strong slicespin on it. That will cause the ball to stop near the hole.

In addressing the ball, which should be played midway between your feet in a very open stance, be sure your hands are behind it. Make sure, too, to lay the blade of your sand wedge wide open. Tilt your head to your right, away from the target. Because your head weighs about 25 pounds, this tilt will encourage you to stay behind the ball. Pick a spot 1½ inches behind the ball and focus hard on it; that's where you want the clubhead to contact the sand while it's moving at high speed.

Making a loose, sort of carefree backswing motion is very important to setting yourself up for a hard smack of clubhead on sand at impact. So cock your wrists early, then swing the club outside the target line and up to the three-quarter position.

On the way down, keep your head and body *steady* as you whip the club across the target line and hit the sand behind the ball with a strong glancing blow. Keep the follow-through short.

The ball will carry to the plateau and stop quickly next to the pin.

When the ball is near the back wall of a bunker, brace your right leg to promote an upright backswing arc.

87 THE UP-AGAINST-THE-WALL SAND-SAVE

In facing a sand shot from near the back wall of a bunker, many club golfers chip out sideways. I agree that chipping out safely back to the fairway is the sensible solution, if after having assessed the situation you determine that there is truly *no* room to swing—that your club will hit the wall on the backswing. However, if there is sufficient space behind the ball, here's how to recover.

Set up with your hands well forward of the ball and lean your weight heavily left to promote an upright-angled backswing. Bracing your right leg is also a most critical stance for encouraging a vitally important upright swing.

Open the clubface of your sand wedge and keep it open through impact to lift the ball from this very precarious spot.

Next, take the club straight back and up, then, finally, swing sharply down, striking a little nearer to the ball and more deeply under it than you typically do in sand.

TAILORING THE TIP

If there's less than 15 feet of green to work with, you'll need to swing on an out-to-in plane in order to impart soft-landing cutspin on the ball.

88 THE HIT-AND-STOP FROM PACKED SAND

Rain squalls are a common occurrence in Puerto Rico, which makes me extremely qualified to explain how to recover from packed wet sand.

On this shot, you should lay the blade wide open but set it square to the target—don't aim left—as the wet sand will minimize any sidespin put on the ball. Moreover, since the green will be wet, too, its wet grass will nullify even the slightest amount of sidespin that's imparted on the ball.

Whether or not you choke down on the club and take a wide stance is a matter of personal comfort. The choice is yours. However, you'll have to alter your normal explosion technique somewhat to deal with this course condition.

Packed wet sand transmits more force from the clubhead to the ball, necessitating a gentler swing tempo and touch. So swing back more slowly and smoothly than you normally do.

On the downswing, hit slightly closer to the ball than usual and employ a hit-and-stop action, rather than a hit-through action. You'll dig the club's leading edge into the packed wet sand and lift the ball safely out of the bunker.

89 THE OVER-THE-BUNKER-WALL BLAST

Anytime my ball sits nicely in a sand bunker, but very close to a high lip, I concentrate on severely *dipping* my shoulders. This unorthodox swinging

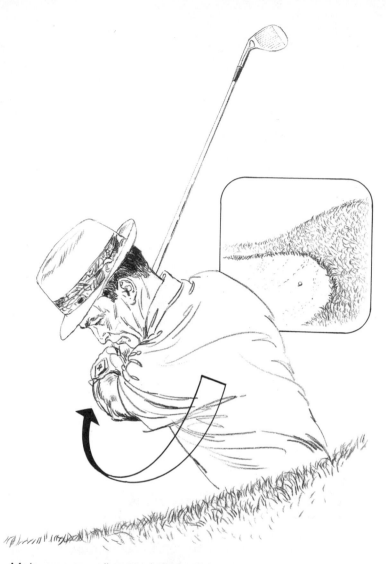

Make sure you dip your left shoulder on the backswing when playing an over-the-bunker-wall blast shot.

action in turn allows me to scoop the ball out, so that it carries over the bunker's wall and stops next to the hole. Here's how to put this shot into your bag.

Assume an open alignment, since that setup allows you to swing the club freely back and through on a steep plane with your arms controlling the motion.

To program high ball flight into your address, play the ball off your left instep and open the face of a sand wedge. Also, grip the club with your right hand turned under the handle (in a strong position) and drop your right shoulder more. Both of these adjustments will allow you to scoop the ball out of the sand more easily, provided you properly employ the dipping action of your shoulders.

Dip your left shoulder immediately on the backswing to send the club flying upward.

Start the downswing by dipping your right shoulder; this helps you keep your weight on your right side as the clubhead drops down into a spot about 2 inches behind the ball. Staying back on your right side is the most vital swing key for producing an extra-high shot. So the higher you need to hit the shot, the more you should dip your right shoulder.

S H O T
90 THE EXTRACTOR

Many country club–level golfers react with panic when they find a ball buried in a sand bunker. The typical high handicapper immediately tenses up and makes a quick swing that's usually bad.

In truth, when the bunker's front lip is low and there's plenty of surface between the edge of the green and the hole, this shot is easy. First, select a pitching wedge. Second, make a compact backswing. Third, make a more *forceful* downswing than usual.

The blade of a sand wedge features bounce, so it

will not extract the ball. The pitching wedge has a sharper blade, so it is the perfect club.

The force of driving the clubhead into the sand, directly at the back of the plug, is enough to pop out the ball. This is why a long follow-through action is not needed.

A proper setup, however, is more crucial than normal. You must address the ball with an exaggerated open alignment, for that type of position promotes a very short, very steep backswing plane. That, in turn, enables you to smack the sand with a sharp, stunted blow.

SHOT

91 THE KNIFE

Here's a real doozy of a sand shot that you must work very hard to perfect—not because the technique required is overly complex, but rather because the very sharp, *knifelike* impact of club on sand requires absolute precision.

I use this shot on the rare occasion when my ball is buried under the lip of a greenside sand bunker and the pin is cut only about 10 feet into the putting surface.

To hit it, I use a putter—yes, a putter—because even a pitching wedge will not dig deeply enough into the sand. If I used the pitching wedge, I'd fail to produce the height and stopping action I'd need to leave myself an easy-to-convert putt.

When you set up to play the ball, assume an open stance so that your arms will have a free passage to swing the putter back and through. Lean 70

AROUND THE GREEN · 161

When you play a knife shot, pull the club down hard so that its toe-end strikes the sand precisely ½ inch behind the ball.

percent of your weight on your left side and leave it there to encourage a firm downward hit.

Just before you're ready to begin your backswing, check that the toe of the putter (preferably a *thin*-blade type) points at a spot directly behind the ball.

Swing the club on such an upright plane that it virtually points straight up at the sky when you reach the desired halfway position.

Pull the club down hard so that its toe-end strikes the sand precisely ½ inch behind the ball. If you make contact closer behind the ball than that, the ball will roll over the green. If you make contact more than a ½ inch behind the ball, you'll be hitting another shot out of the same bunker.

CHI CHI'S CLINIC

STAY DOWN TO STOP TOPPING

If you top short pitch shots from greenside grass bunkers you probably stand up before the ball is struck. You see, if the club is soled flush behind the ball at address, any lifting thereafter will naturally cause the club to lift up, too. Therefore, the thin leading edge, rather than the sweet spot of the clubface, catches the ball. This poor contact usually causes the ball to run over the green.

To cure this problem, try to maintain your knee flex and keep your eye on the ball as long as possible. Because both your upper body and lower body will now stay down, you'll hit a pure pitch.

FINE TUNE YOUR TOUCH

To fine tune your touch for playing a delicate pitch, which is a common greenside shot, set a basket on your lawn 5 yards away from you and practice hitting balls into it.

Practice this drill daily for only a half hour and you'll truly sharpen your hand-eye coordination and increase your feel for the clubhead.

I recommend you use a brush mat to hit from; otherwise, you might ruin your lawn.

FEEL IS IN YOUR FINGERTIPS

On greenside chips, feel transmitted through your fingers is much more important because you're trying to hit the ball close to the cup, as opposed to just trying to hit the fairway on a tee-shot or a green with a long approach.

To enhance feel, make sure that the tips of your fingers—especially your right thumb and right forefinger—are lightly touching. Maintain that connection throughout the stroke and you'll find you have more control over the shot, since the right hand is the closest to the clubhead.

LET THE CLUB DO THE WORK

Golfers who misdirect chips often do so because they try to help the ball up into the air. Don't make the same mistake; use a good left hand-wrist-arm guiding action through impact and let the loft of the club fly the ball onto the green toward the hole.

Here's how to rehearse and memorize a firm left-sided chipping action: Hit some chips with a seven-iron under a standard four-legged chair. The idea is to fly the ball through both sets of legs without hitting any part of the chair. (If you can't hit the ball under the chair consistently, you're using too much right hand.) Practice until you feel confident about hitting the shot.

CHIP IT CLOSE

Many players with whom I've played in Pro-Ams hit chip shots well past the hole. I think that's because they concentrate so hard on direction and so little on gauging distance.

To help you hit the ball the correct distance, within easy one-putt range, try to roll the ball to a small imaginary circle around the hole.

OPEN SAYS ME

On most sand shots you need to open the clubface. However, unless you are a totally intuitive player, you should open the clubface of a sand wedge a particular number of degrees, according to the height of the lip, before entering the bunker. (Generally, the higher the lip, the more you should open the clubface.) That way, you'll have a steady, more systematic gauge, that will allow you to cut out the precise amount of sand.

BRUSH THE BILL

To help you scalp the right amount of sand on normal bunker shots, try imagining a dollar bill a couple of inches or so below the surface of the sand, under the ball. Then, when you hit, try to brush the top of the bill from end to end with the bottom of the clubhead.

5

ON THE GREEN

Prior to playing a round of golf, I hit shots on the practice tee, mainly to get a sense of feel for the clubhead. After hitting about thirty-five to fifty balls with a variety of clubs, I know how well my swing is working. On any given day, therefore, I can pretty much foretell what number of drives I'll hit in the fairway and how many greens I'll reach in regulation figures with my approach shots. Conversely, following a preround putting session, I still have no clue at all about how well things are going to go on the greens during play, even if I holed everything in practice. That, my golfing amigos, is how crazy this *ground game* is.

Putting reminds me of a unique coin, with a heavenly side and a hellish side. I say this because a day on the greens is generally either especially satisfying or extremely agonizing, depending on whether I make or miss the majority of putts over eighteen holes. Also, and maybe more important, the simple-looking act of stroking a golf ball into a small hole depends about as much on luck as it does on skill. That's because in any very finely manicured and seemingly billiard-tablelike green, there are subtle imperfections in the surface that are not immediately visible, but that affect the roll of the ball (in addition to the spike marks and repaired ball mark spots we are all familiar with). This is why my good friend Gary Player considers putting an inexact science.

Regardless of the role luck plays in putting, I know from hard experience that technique, touch, and temperament are still very important.

I used to think that in order for a player to putt well he always had to adhere to a set of principles. Namely, play the ball off the sweet spot of the putter, use an arm-and-shoulder controlled wristless stroke, and keep the putterblade moving low to the ground during the backstroke and downstroke. However, I've since altered my putting philosophy. Too many good putters violate these so-called laws. Furthermore, I myself continue to experience good success on the greens, owing to an unorthodox wristy method I learned a few years ago. (I'll get more into that stroke when I discuss the 20-foot hole-hunter.)

In spite of how important it is to be able to repeat a good stroke, I'm convinced that many requirements for fine putting concern the equipment you use, your prestroke routine, and your mental frame of mind—elements well outside the realm of putting technique.

A good-looking, good-feeling putter is an obvious requirement for good putting. Reading line and grain are also important to holing out consistently. However, that's not enough. Before you actually swing the putter, you must concentrate so intensely on a line you have visualized in advance that you see the ball roll along it and into the hole.

Then there is the element of mental attitude. You must be patient enough to accept that perfectly stroked putts hit along the correct line don't always drop into the cup. Also, you must always maintain the high degree of confidence that comes from steady practice.

You must stay calm, too. Never overreact to a putt you hole or a putt you miss. Do that and the tempo of your stroke will be thrown out of sync. When that happens, you hit the ball well by or well short of the hole, through the break, or short of a crest in the green where the break begins. The list of errors goes on. In short, you miss putts.

To summarize: Play with a putter that is esthetically appealing and feels good; assume a comfortable setup; use a natural-feeling personalized stroke; carefully read line and grain; keep a cool head and calm heart; and maintain a high level of confidence.

Now that you've grasped my ground-level putting philosophy, you're ready to learn the fine points.

SHOT
92 THE PERFECT LAG

To prevent three-putt greens from wrecking your score, you should be prepared to putt on large greens, where putts over 35 feet in length are very common.

On such lengthy putts, particularly over icelike surfaces, *two-putting* should be your only objective. If the ball you're lagging happens to drop into the hole, that's a bonus.

In preparing to putt a *snake,* as long putts are called, visualize how fast your ball must roll along

Standing tall to the ball by flexing your knees less than normal will promote a perfect lag-putting stroke.

a particular line to give you the perfect distance. Then translate this speed into feel; determine how long a stroke you must make.

Unless the green is severely sloped, speed should be your priority on long putts. Your major goal should be to drop the ball into an imaginary 2-foot circle anywhere around the hole.

Once you've calculated the speed, straighten up in relation to the putt in order to encourage a smooth, highly controlled stroke. Standing more upright will also enhance your perspective of the line and your feel for the distance.

Swing the putterblade low to the ground, going back and going through, using an almost totally arms-shoulders action. To make this stroke work, you must keep your head and body perfectly still.

Be smart: Trade some playing time for practicing long putts. Such practice will help you determine the precise length of stroke to employ for a required distance, will teach you how to deal with different surfaces, and will help you to ingrain a nice rhythm in your muscle-memory.

SHOT
93 THE OFF-THE-TOE PUTT

Putting over a speedy surface is tricky enough, but factor in a downhill slope and you've got a situation requiring a sure touch and unique technique. The slightest flaw in your strategy or stroke will cause a three-putt.

In order to stroke this type of putt into the hole from a short distance or close to it from more than 20 feet away, try addressing the ball slightly toward the toe of the putter. This produces a dead type of hit. You can hit the ball more firmly off the putter-blade's toe-end, and the ball will not roll as far as it would have if you had stroked it with the club's sweet spot. Because of this technique, you will address each downhill putt with added confidence—something every golfer needs on the greens to hole out in low numbers.

TAILORING THE TIP

Hitting off the toe can cause the blade to open at impact. If you carry a light putter, guard against this happening by gripping the handle firmly with both hands.

SHOT

94 THE PUNCHED PUTT

· ·

When it's very gusty on the course (conditions particularly common to Florida, Texas, Scotland, and Puerto Rico) golfers often putt poorly because the wind interferes with their sense of balance during their stroke.

You won't experience this problem if you crouch at address. Crouching lowers your center of gravity, thus your setup becomes rock-solid secure and allows you to stroke the ball solidly.

Widening your stance by a couple of inches so that the heels of your shoes are outside your shoulder blades will also be of great benefit when putting in extremely high wind.

Choking down on the putter will increase your stroke control.

On the backstroke you can increase your control even more by fixing your eyes on the ball and keeping the motion short.

On the through stroke, sort of punch the ball in the hitting area, keeping a firm grip on the handle. The faster roll you'll put on the ball will send it spinning more truly to the cup, thus it will be a rare wind that blows it off its line.

SHOT
95 THE TOPPER

When I'm putting uphill on a sluggish putting surface I first imagine a second hole directly behind the one I'm aiming for. Doing this helps me hit the ball up near the hole—if not into it—which is a plus on long putts.

Another good tip for putting uphill over slow surfaces is to hit more of the top half of the ball, which *lessens* the backspin imparted to it. Consequently, the putt rolls truer, holding its line much longer than a weakly hit ball does.

In pool, hitting the top half of a ball imparts topspin. Apply the same principle when playing a "topper" and you'll never leave a ball short on a slow green.

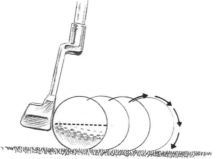

96 THE RIGHT-TO-LEFT SINKER

Psychologically, right-to-left putts used to bother me much more than left-to-right breakers. Maybe it was my imagination, but I thought the ball moved faster down the slope on right-to-left putts. Therefore, I'd frequently decelerate the putterblade in the hitting area for fear of going well by the hole—and finish up hitting the ball miles off-line, on the low side of the cup.

Nowadays, I'm a changed putter. I see the putt breaking from right-to-left and rolling into the hole before I even stroke. I'm more confident, and my putting action is less tentative. However, in addition to thinking more positively and making a more accelerating stroke, here's my biggest lesson to you for holing more right-to-left putts: *Play the ball closer to your right foot.*

That unique setup will enable you to swing out at the putt—in the direction the ball should start rolling. Don't ever make the mistake of playing the ball up in your stance, otherwise you'll probably never start the ball on the right line.

One secret to sinking a right-to-left breaking putt is to play the ball nearer your right foot.

97 THE LEFT-TO-RIGHT SINKER

On a left-to-right sharp breaking putt, you want the ball to start travelling on a line left of the hole, what golfers call the high side. Moving the ball *forward* in your stance (i.e., off your left instep) enables you to contact the ball late in the forward stroke, when the putterface has closed slightly, thereby ensuring that you start the ball left of the hole. The bigger the slope, break, or burrow in the green, the further you should play the ball up in your stance.

To further encourage putting the ball on the high-side line to the hole, assume an open stance. After setting up with the putterface aimed left of the hole, swing smoothly back.

On the downstroke, keep your head perfectly still and allow the putterblade to close naturally. Lift your head when you hear the ball ring the metal cup!

98 THE DEW-GOODER

When morning dew blankets a green, guard against three-putting by making two simple technical changes.

Because the dew on the surface of the grass stops the ball from following the natural contour of the green, you must allow for *half* of the usual amount of break. In other words, if it normally looks like you'll have to start the putt 6 inches outside the right of the hole, allow for it to only break 3 inches on dewy greens.

Now, just go ahead and give the ball a more solid rap, hitting it with a *hooded* putterblade so it nicely holds its line.

99 THE ACCELERATOR STROKE

On Bermuda greens the ball rolls considerably more slowly and breaks less because of the heavy-textured blades of grass. Those of you who putt these surfaces at home or while vacationing should allow for changes in speed and burrow. Also, you should contemplate changing your putter or its characteristics. You may even want to kick around the idea of altering your setup and stroke.

A heavier putter will impart more roll to the ball, thus ensuring that you hit the ball up to the hole on these coarse surfaces. You might want to look for a new model putter in your local pro shop. My advice to those of you who would rather not even retire temporarily "old reliable": either add some lead tape to it or change your technique.

You can change your swing by simply widening your stance by several inches. Standing with your feet spread further apart promotes a *longer take-away* action, which then prompts you to accelerate the blade more on the through stroke automatically.

100 THE 20-FOOT HOLE-HUNTER

Since joining the Senior Tour in late 1985, I've won a bundle of money. The reason, in a nutshell, is that I'm holing 20-footers more than ever before in my career.

I credit my newfound success on the greens to a unique yet simple right-handed stroke I learned in early 1986 from Billy Casper, a fellow senior player who is one of golf's all-time great putters. Casper sets up with both the butt-end of the putter and the back of his left hand resting against his left thigh. He raises the putterblade rather high off the ground on the backstroke by cocking his right wrist. He then gently snaps the putterface into the ball by uncocking his right wrist at the start of the downstroke. The whole action works with the steady rhythm of car pistons going up and down. And once contact is made, the ball seems to *hunt* the hole.

I guess I'm living proof that you can teach an old dog new tricks. Unless you are putting the eyes out of the hole already, this is one technique you should surely experiment with.

101 THE SHORT PUTT CONVERTER

Many amateur golfers who face a very short putt in a big club match or big Nassau bet often crack under pressure. The typical "yipper" so much fears missing a kneeknocker that he makes a sloppy backstroke, then stabs at the ball wildly with the putterface.

I'm no sports psychologist, so I can't tell you precisely why players who are successful positive thinkers in the real world talk themselves into missing short putts out on the golf course. But I can tell you that confidence—believing you will hole

You'll knock in more kneeknockers if you keep the backstroke short and aim to hit an imaginary backstop behind the hole.

the putt—is one major key to success on the greens. So before you start your stroke, replay some of those past putts you've knocked in the hole under pressure.

Now that you've got things squared away between your ears, here's a physical tip that will help you convert more short putts.

After assuming a comfortable but fundamentally sound setup, swing the putterhead back slowly into an imaginary backstop. Then encourage a solid through stroke by imagining that there is a *backstop* directly behind the hole.

CHI CHI'S CLINIC

HIT THE BALL WITH THE PUTTER'S SWEET SPOT

Contacting the ball with the sweet spot of the putter's face will produce the purest roll; therefore, unless you are trying to take some speed off the putt by hitting the ball with the toe of the putter, or trying to add velocity by purposely hitting the top half of the ball, always make contact with the sweet spot.

Most putters on the market feature a line, or a marking of some sort, indicating the position of the sweet spot. If you like the look and feel of an old putter that has no such mark, make your own by filing a groove in the top of the putterhead or painting a line there.

To find the sweet spot, hold the putter very lightly between your thumb and forefinger, at the top of the handle, so that the club hangs vertically with the blade facing you. Now, with a coin tap the putter at different spots on its face. When you miss the sweet spot, the putterhead will wobble. When you hit the sweet spot, the impact will feel solid and the blade will swing straight back and then straight toward you.

IS YOUR STROKE SWEET?

Putts hit off-line or short of the hole could indicate that you're missing the sweet spot. To test your impact point, dip a ball in a glass of water, then putt it across a green. Look at the putterface and you'll see exactly where contact was made. If you're off the sweet spot mark, make some adjustments in your setup and stroke until you are on the mark.

HOW TO PLUMB BOB PUTTS

If you ever have trouble determining the subtle breaks in a green, try plumb bobbing the line. Here's how this system works: Stand directly behind the ball with your feet spread shoulder-width and the putter held in front of you. The cup, ball, and one eye should all be aligned. You should hold the putter's handle lightly between your right thumb and forefinger (left-handed putters should reverse the instructions) so that it hangs at arm's length straight down in front of you.

Sighting with your eye, angle the putter so the lowest point of the shaft covers the ball. Next, while keeping your head perfectly still, look up at the hole. If the hole becomes visible to the right of the shaft, the ground slopes left to right; if it appears to the left, the ground slopes right to left. If the hole is directly in line with the shaft, the ground is level.

Plumb bobbing works best on putts of 20 feet or less because the further you stand from the hole, the greater the chance that the slope where you stand and the slope around the hole are different.

READ THE GRAIN

If you are reading the break of the green correctly, aligning the putter and your body properly, and employing a sound stroke, yet still missing putts frequently, you could be failing to take into account the effects of grain.

If the green has a shiny look, the grain is running toward the hole, thus you should stroke the ball a tad easier.

If the green's surface is dull, the grain is running toward you, a sure sign that you must stroke more firmly to reach the hole.

HEAD GAMES

To learn the knack of keeping your head steady, which is paramount to developing a sound repeatable stroke, place a ball about three inches from the base of your living-room wall. Rest your head gently against the wall, then swing the blade back and through, keeping the toe-end of the blade very close to the wall.

BUILD ACCELERATION INTO YOUR PUTTING ACTION

On medium-length putts, some players swing the putterblade back correctly, a bit inside the target line, but push the ball to the right of the hole because they decelerate the blade in the hitting area. Decelerating causes the blade to be left open at impact.

If you think this is your fault, correct it by trying to return the right palm to a square position (facing the hole) through impact. This reminder, plus the two practice tips that follow, will encourage good acceleration and allow you to hit more on-line putts.

TIP ONE: *Line up two balls a couple of inches apart along a particular line. Only if the first ball is struck solidly will the second ball be hit squarely.*

Practicing this drill for ten minutes a day for a week will cure you of your tentative stroke.

TIP TWO: *Weight your putter by adding strips of lead tape to the back of its head. Then practice your stroke.*

After just a week of practice remove the tape. You'll see how easily your arms and shoulders work the blade through impact and how many more putts you sink on the golf course.

ALIGN TO ANOTHER TARGET

If you ever have trouble setting up squarely to the hole on a very long putt, pick out an interim spot along the correct line a few feet in front of the ball. Then set the putterface square to it. After that, simply roll the ball over the spot and it will find its way to the cup.

LIGHTEN UP

Feel is more critical on long putts than on short ones; therefore, if you're lagging putts well short of the hole, you're probably holding the club's handle too tightly.

To determine if this is your fault, have your playing partner try to pull the putter out of your hands before your preround practice of long putts. If the pressure in your fingers is okay, your buddy should feel only a little resistance. If he has to tug, that's your sign to grip the club more lightly.

THE NOSE KNOWS

Many players who pull putts look up before the ball has been struck.

Anxious eyes cause the shoulders to move out of a square position parallel to the putting line. This fault, in turn, causes the putterblade to point well left of the hole at impact, which unfortunately is the direction the ball rolls.

To remedy this fault, or to guard against it, set up with your nose aligned with the ball. Then once you stroke wait until you hit the ball before you look up.

BEAT THE KNEEKNOCKER BLUES

Holing kneeknockers is critical to scoring, so here are two exercises that should help you become a putting machine.

INDOOR DRILL: *Each evening putt twenty straight putts into a bedpost 3 feet away before retiring. In addition to heightening your feel and building your confidence, this exercise will help you deal with pressure.*

OUTDOOR DRILL: *Put a tee-peg into the practice green and putt to it from 3 feet away. Practice this for an hour so that when you get to the course the 4¼-inch hole looks like a well.*

NO STRINGS ATTACHED

This will surprise you, but one of the best ways to improve your short and long putting is with a 10-foot piece of string.

SHORT PUTTS: *Run the string from a level spot on the practice green to a hole 10 feet away. Tack the string down from the spot you picked to the front of the hole. Then, simply putt the ball along the string. You'll find that you'll concentrate harder on the line and make a much better stroke.*

LONG PUTTS: *Stretch a string horizontally on an area of the practice putting green where there is no hole nearby. Remember, on long putts you want to be more distance conscious than hole conscious. You want to lag the ball close enough for an easy conversion. So to enhance your touch from the range around 35 to 50 feet, pace practice putts just short of the string, as if you were pitching pennies to a wall.*

CHI CHI RODRIGUEZ:
A PROFILE

BORN: October 23, 1935, in Rio Pidras, Puerto Rico
HEIGHT: 5 feet 7½ inches
WEIGHT: 132 pounds
FAMILY: wife, Iwalani; daughter, Donnette
RESIDENCE: Naples, Florida
SPECIAL INTERESTS: Underprivileged children,
    boxing, pool, baseball
TURNED PROFESSIONAL: 1960
JOINED PGA TOUR: 1960
JOINED SENIOR PGA TOUR: 1985
ATTACHMENTS: Equinus Greens, Orlando, Florida;
    Dorado Sands, Dorado, Puerto Rico

PGA TOUR VICTORIES

1963: Denver Open
1964: Lucky International; Western Open
1967: Texas Open
1968: Sahara Invitational
1972: Byron Nelson Classic
1973: Greater Greensboro Open
1979: Tallahassee Open

PGA TOUR CAREER EARNINGS: $1,037,105

INTERNATIONAL APPEARANCES:

Member 1973 Ryder Cup Team; represented Puerto Rico on twelve World Cup teams

SENIOR PGA TOUR VICTORIES*

1986: Senior Tournament Players Championship
Digital Seniors Classic
United Virginia Bank Seniors

1987: General Foods PGA Seniors Championship
Vantage at the Dominion
United Hospitals Senior Golf Championship
Silver Pages Classic
Senior Players Reunion Pro-Am
Digital Seniors Classic
GTE Northwest Classic

1988: Doug Sanders Kingwood Celebrity Classic
Digital Seniors Classic

1989: Crestar Classic

CURRENT SENIOR PGA TOUR EARNINGS: $1,440,321

INTERNATIONAL SENIOR GOLF VICTORIES

1988: Japan Pro Senior Championship

HONORS

1974: Charlie Bartlett Award, from the Golf Writer's Association of America for unselfish contributions to the betterment of society

1981: Richardson Award, from the Golf Writer's Association of America to recognize an individual who has consistently made an outstanding contribution to golf

* Chi Chi won both the 1988 and 1989 Senior Skins, earning a total of $420,000.

1981: Ambassador of Golf Award, World Series of Golf annually recognizes someone who has fostered ideals of game on international level and whose concern for others extends beyond the golf course

1982: Father of the Year Award

1986: Card Walker Award, for outstanding contribution to Junior Golf

1987: National Puerto Rican Coalition Life Achievement Award

Gold Tee Award, from the Metropolitan Golf Writer's Association to recognize an individual who has contributed to the good of the game over a long period of time.

Senior Player of the Year

Byron Nelson Award, for the low stroke average on the Senior PGA Tour

Arnold Palmer Award, given to the leading money winner on the Senior PGA Tour

1988: Old Tom Morris Award, for his lifetime commitment to golf and helping to mold the welfare of the game in a manner of style exemplified by Old Tom Morris

1988: Fred Raphael Award, for exceptional service to the game

1989: Bob Jones Award, the highest honor bestowed by the United States Golf Association, honoring the cause of fair play that was exemplified by the late Robert Tyre Jones